Fen Boy First

Edward Storey was born at Whittlesey in the Isle of Ely and the area has been his home ever since. He is an established poet and has published five collections of verse. His topographical writings include *Portrait of the Fen Country*, *Four Seasons in Three Countries*, *Spirit of the Fens*, *Summer Journeys through the Fens*, *The Solitary Landscape* and *The Winter Fens*.

Fen Boy First

EDWARD STOREY

ROBERT HALE · LONDON

ISBN 0 7090 5454 8

Robert Hale Limited
Clerkenwell House
Clerkenwell Green
London EC1R 0HT

2 4 6 8 10 9 7 5 3 1

Photoset in North Wales by
Derek Doyle & Associates, Mold, Clwyd.
Printed in Great Britain by
St Edmundsbury Press Limited, Bury St Edmunds, Suffolk.
Bound by WBC Limited, Bridgend, Glamorgan.

Contents

Illustrations

Acknowledgements

One or two brief episodes in this autobiography have appeared in different forms, in previous publications, but now take their correct place in the chronology of their happening. Some of the poems have also appeared in magazines or on television programmes and I wish to thank the editors and producers of *Cambridgeshire Pride, the Countryman, Envoi, Outposts, Proof, Vision On,* and London Weekend Television's *The South Bank Show.* I am also grateful to the many people who have been kind enough to talk to me about their own memories of the years with which this volume is concerned.

for Angela

1930–35

1 Where I watched the darkness

My father lifted me up to look over the wall of the brickyard kiln where he worked and pointed to the distant lights of Peterborough pin-pricking the horizon. Seeing them across the low, flat fields already darkened by the sky, they seemed to belong to another country. And when my father said in his flat, tired voice, 'One day you might go there', he made it sound like the end of a lifetime's adventure which only a few achieved.

That faraway city, so I thought, was a place where there were no bricks, clay, smudge or smoke; no burnt hands or backs, or weariness and sweat. It was a place where everything would be different, where the setting sun was no longer barricaded beyond my reach by the tall chimneys of the brickworks.

Peterborough was only four miles from King's Dyke where my father worked as a burner, and King's Dyke was less than two miles from my home-town of Whittlesey. But the distance was enough to separate the known from the unknown as much as any uncharted ocean.

A prehistoric sea had once covered the land over which I looked and its deposits had formed the blue clay from which the brick industry had grown. The spirit of that sea was still there.

Our world was bricks. Rows of bricks like ancient cliffs out of which someone had made rooms which we called houses. We were like martins disappearing from the street through little openings into those hidden nesting-places where we lived.

Whittlesey was encircled then by more than a hundred tall chimneys which squeezed their sulphurous smoke into the sky, as if the air so high up was always frosty. Below them were the black, fortress-like kilns where clay was fashioned and fired into bricks for the rest of England. My grandfather, who worked for a time in the early days of the brickyards, used to say he helped to build London. I did not take it as a light-hearted boast.

We lived in Church Street, in a two-up, two-down terraced house with a bucket lavatory half way down the garden path, which was also shared by our neighbours. It had an ill-fitting stable door which offered few privacies and failed completely to keep out the north wind in winter. It was a dingy place and I tried not to visit it too often.

Wherever you lived in Whittlesey the brickyards impinged on your life as much as the land and harvest did on that other major provider – farming. If bricks dominated our world to the west of the town, then the fens to the east were to have an ever-increasing influence on me as I grew up and explored their vastness and history.

But, before I took that open landscape for granted, I was for the first three or four years of my life much more aware of the life in our street, where men came home each day from work, their boots caked with red dust, their shirts rusty with sweat, their hands and backs blistered from the fierce heat of the kilns. Clay-getter, smudger, burner, presser and drawer, were classifications as common as butcher, cobbler, horse-keeper and rent-collector.

Like coal-mining, the brickyards were not without their dangers and accidents. Often workers were injured when bricks collapsed in the chambers where they had been fired. Burns were frequent and deaths not unknown. Men had been scarred or crippled for life. 'And yet', my father often recalled long after he'd worked there, 'during the Depression men queued all day for jobs like that, and if the foreman didn't think you were pulling your weight someone else would soon take your place ... We had to wear wet sacks over our backs to stop them from blistering, and the sacks would be parched on your skin before you got out of the chamber with your tally ...'

My father's job was to feed the fires in the chambers where the bricks were baked until the heart of the kiln was pre-Genesis white. The heat was awesome. He was in charge of the kiln and had a small brick hut at the base of the hundred-foot high shaft where he sat and brewed tea in a large brown enamel pot. Although he was quite a big man he looked dwarfed by the chimney. With his cloth cap at a tilt over his dirty face he could have been mistaken for an unkempt gnome in some sunless, fairy-tale world where children only had nightmares.

My visits to the kiln are among my earliest recollections and yet I don't suppose that I went all that often. I do remember being taken in my push-chair, with my sister Freda – who was five years older – walking beside me. The reason for these trips was so that mother could take an evening meal to my father when he had to work a double-shift in order to change from a week of day-work to a week of nights.

I suppose these visits must have been mostly in summer when it was light until late evening, but the occasions that stand out most clearly are the ones where I watched the darkness creep over the earth and saw the distant lights of a city. As well as those lights I remember the sunsets when a large crimson ball of fire squatted on the horizon and I feared the world would melt in its ferocity.

I also remember the walks home, past the railway-crossing and the houses of King's Dyke (built by the brickyard owners), past the Mile Tree and the recreation field with its tall water-tower, past Mr Bingham's mill and the *Packhorse Inn*, until we turned into our own yard with its iron water-pump outside our back door, and then into the warm shadows of our kitchen where we were given a quick wash before being put to bed.

I cannot remember whether I dreamt of the fierce fires in the kiln or the distant glimmering lights of Peterborough, but I do know that I was always glad to wake up on Monday mornings to the smell of wash-day, with its soap-suds, steaming copper, and white sheets blowing on the line.

My mother, I know, hated these double shifts which father had to work, not only because it meant another nine or ten hours without him, but also because some of the worst accidents happened when the men were working that extra shift and were very tired. The long walk home to an empty house left her silent for most of the way and it would not be long before she followed her children to bed.

These memories were brought back to me recently by the

discovery of an old shoe-box full of black-and-white snapshots taken more than fifty years ago. I was helping my brother and sister to clear the house where my parents had spent their last thirty years together and, in one of the bedroom cupboards, were boxes of press-cuttings of births, deaths, marriages and anniversaries, together with old post-cards and the photographs. The corners of the shoe-box were broken and the lid was kept on by an elastic band. Even the price of the shoes was still marked on the side. How much was seven shillings and eleven pence? And when? And, I ask myself, how old are we before we realize that there was a time before we were born, that life existed before us?

There were photographs of events long before I was born in 1930 and most of them were dated. One was for August 1912, when the harvest-fields were flooded and men stood knee-deep in water, gathering in the stooks. Punts were being used instead of horses and carts and a pencilled note on the back said that my grandfather was third on the left.

There was another photograph of the peace celebrations in 1919, at the unveiling of the war memorial for all those men killed in the Great War. It looked as if half the population of Whittlesey had gathered on the market-place for the ceremony, the women in long black dresses and straw hats; the men in cloth caps or bowlers, and the children in knickerbockers or pinafores. Near the Buttercross someone was waving and smiling at the camera.

How many of those townspeople are alive now? And what of all those events that were never recorded by a camera – the stories that became legends round winter fires centuries ago? All towns absorb something of the past. To begin a life-story of anyone is to start halfway because what we are goes back to long before we drew our first breath.

I was born on 28 February at two minutes to midnight. My parents were always very precise about the time because I was to keep them awake during many midnights after my initial cries shattered their candle-lit bedroom. It was a cold night, my mother often told me, with the window-blinds pulled down and the curtains drawn, as much to keep out the frosty air as to hide what was happening in the room.

There was no heating upstairs and, at that time, no gas or electric light either. Whilst Dr Bernard and the midwife attended to me, my father and sister sat downstairs waiting for the news. A few hours later my grandmother arrived to take over and father went off to work.

That bedroom, with its red-rose wallpaper and cracked ceiling, was to become a very familiar part of the house to me during my childhood for I was to spend several weeks of each year in it when I was entertaining one of the many illnesses I attracted – asthma, bronchitis, measles, double pneumonia, whooping-cough, chicken-pox and croup. Fortunately I did not become a victim of diphtheria which was something that afflicted numerous children in the town. Week after week the doctor called as regularly as the milk-girl, baker, rent-collector and insurance agent. Hours were punctuated not so much by the chiming clock on the wall as by the clink of medicine-bottles, and the weary steps of my mother climbing the narrow, twisting stairs to my room, which was also theirs.

The steps I did not welcome were those of my father as he came up to apply another linseed-oil-and-mustard poultice to my chest. I tried to stifle my screams as the fiery concoction was placed on me, then made firm by a sheet of brown paper and a red flannelette vest. Afterwards, when my crying subsided, mother sat on the bed and sang to me –

> *Ride a cock-horse to Banbury Cross.*
> *To see a fine lady upon a white horse;*
> *With rings on her fingers and bells on her toes,*
> *She shall have music wherever she goes.*

She always rhymed *Cross* with *horse*, just as she always rhymed *vase* with *gauze*, as most local people did. Later, when I had calmed down, my parents came to bed, often sleeping either side of me rather than putting me into a cold cot.

My mother was a small woman, pretty in a plain kind of way – pretty and strong. Before her marriage she had worked on the land, doing every job but beet-chopping. Her father had been killed on a farm when he was only twenty-six and she was three. From then on she was brought up by her grandmother who lived in Claygate, Whittlesey. Her own mother re-married and went to live in the village of

Sawtry, near Huntingdon which was always spoken of as 'somewhere beyond the Great North Road' and, consequently, the two women saw little of each other. They met no more than twice a year and that was when my 'grandma from Sawtry' came to see us.

I realize now that my mother must have had a brief and impoverished childhood for she left school when she was only thirteen and went to work full-time in the fields. Six years later she married my father and began her own family, which was not without its setbacks – her first-born dying when he was only two years old.

As a girl she was sent to the Congregational Sunday School where she met my father. They became childhood sweethearts and that chapel was to be their place of worship for most of their sixty-three years of marriage.

One of the photographs I found in the shoe-box was of her taken just before she was married. She was probably eighteen at the time and wearing a silk dress with a large bow. She could have been painted by Vermeer or Chardin. I never saw her look like this. To me she was always a woman busy in the kitchen, or the wash-house – scrubbing, ironing or cooking, or looking after me during another illness. She was neither young, nor old, but like my father – ageless –

> I think today of one who
> even before her childhood was quite done
>   worked in the fields in frost and sun
> from day's first light until the moon
>   sent labourers home, the girls
> to mend torn garments in a lamp-lit room
> made private by the pulling down of blinds.
>
> Then, when the cockerels called
> or neighbours knocked upon her window-pane,
>   she went with others just as young
> back to the farm, her slender form
>   ill-matched for such long toil,
> having no time to watch the tall
>   slow cumulus, or hear the skylark's dirl.
>
> And yet through her I love this land
> where less appeals to unperceiving eyes
>   than what I find. I know I take

the aches and elements at second-hand
   and should regret that she
was forced by circumstance to break
her spirit where I forge my song. But who

   will understand the meaning of
my labours now unless they honour hers?
   She would be quick to contradict
my pity and explain in simple terms
   that others had fared worse.
She kept her thoughts like secrets in a house
where sorrow should be patched behind closed doors.

In fact I began these reminiscences mainly because of something my mother said to me just before she died. She was asking me where my wife and I were going for our holidays that year and I told her, Switzerland. She looked at me from an inner distance I had not noticed before. 'Switzerland? What on earth do you want to go there for?'

'Because we like being in the mountains for a change.'

'I don't know why you want to go to the mountains. You'll always be a fen boy first.'

Perhaps she was right and I have no wish to contradict her. Her words reminded me of the story of a Norfolk gentleman telling his gardener that he proposed taking the family on holiday to France that year. The shocked gardener shook his head and said 'But yew've bin to Norwich and Lowestoft, what yew want to goo all foreign for?'

Apart from the nursery rhymes I learnt from my mother, some of the earliest verses I was to know by heart came from the poker-work texts which hung on the bedroom walls. At the top of the stairs was the picture of a hill with the stark outline of a cross against a crude sunset. Underneath were the words –

> *So I'll cherish the old rugged Cross*
> *Till Life's trophies at last I lay down;*
> *I will cling to the old rugged Cross*
> *And exchange it some day for a crown.*

Next to the wardrobe was a dramatic version of the Cross garlanded with flowers and a half-naked woman clinging to it in a distressed state of passion and awe. Her long black hair mesmerized me for weeks and possibly made me more aware of our physical longings than our spiritual ones. But I also learnt that verse off by heart –

> *Rock of Ages, cleft for me,*
> *Let me hide myself in Thee;*
> *Let the water and the blood*
> *From Thy riven side which flowed,*
> *Be of sin the double cure,*
> *Cleanse me from its guilt and power.*

Such verses conditioned my ear not only to rhythm but also to rhyme and near-rhyme: *blood/flow'd, cure/power*; and I derived considerable delight simply from saying words like *riven* without knowing what they meant. At least the hymns I learnt as a child were written by competent verse-makers if not great poets and I remember being particularly moved by the language of 'When I Survey the Wond'rous Cross' even though I had no conception of its religious meaning. Religion, like politics, was never far from our back door and I grew up in a house where we said grace before meals (however inadequate) and knelt down to say our prayers before getting into bed. We went to chapel three times on Sundays and, on that day, were not allowed to play with any of our toys. Above the bed in which I was to spend so much of my childhood, was a picture of *The Last Supper*, a garish imitation of the famous Leonardo da Vinci, but it was considered the most precious thing we possessed. My parents were also very devoted to something called a 'Promise Box', a small casket which contained a selection of biblical texts in the form of small paper scrolls which were picked out at random by a pair of tweezers – a kind of religious bran-tub or lucky dip designed to give you consolation, hope, or inspiration.

The rest of the bedroom was cramped with a chest of drawers, an old dressing-table, a wicker chair, and a wooden blanket chest under the window. The floor had no carpet then but was covered with brown linoleum (a word I could never say as a child and struggle over even now). The ceiling

was almost as brown, patterned as it was with large dark
stains from where the rain came in. Sometimes we had to
place bowls and buckets about the room to catch the water
which, in bad weather, poured through the cracks. Urgent
appeals to our landlord resulted in emergency repairs but it
was like trying to tar over the holes of a sinking ship. The
whole terrace where we lived was 'condemned' before my
parents rented it in 1923, but it was not pulled down until
1957.

I recently came across a copy of a local newspaper dated 21
February 1936 in which there was this report –

A condemned cell is light, dry, airy and clean. A condemned
house in this town boasts none of these desirable features. It is
damp, dark and dismal. It has four rooms. The roof offers
some protection against the elements but has to admit defeat
when the rain, which was intended to soften the earth, pierces
its frail shell and softens the bedclothes. Father and mother,
and four children, are housed under this 'hospitable roof'. So
'hospitable' that, open to the heavens as it is in places, it
permits pools of water, dust and sickness to lodge beneath its
worn thatch ... When will the housing committee begin to see
the suffering due to the demoralizing conditions under which
these people are forced to live in this town?

It's a wonder that the reporter was not thrown into jail for
criticising the town elders like that; perhaps he was, on a
charge of sedition or treason, for in those days local
newspapers were much more aware of who they could, or
should not, offend. For all I know that reporter's words went
unread, for our houses were to stay in that 'hospitable' state
for another twenty years and his description fitted so well the
house where I grew up. And yet, it is a house that I still
remember with affection for within its outward squalidness I
received much love, warmth and happiness. I knew of
nothing better and we were no doubt more fortunate than
many. There was a richness of experience there that makes it
worth writing about now and the one thing I was sure of as a
child was that, however far I might venture from the house in
the years to come, there would always be someone there
when I returned.

Before my parents went to live there my great-grandparents had been its tenants. Then, home-cured hams hung on the whitewashed walls and strings of onions were nailed on the doorposts. The downstairs rooms were lit by oil-lamps, the upstairs ones by candles. The water-supply was the iron pump outside the back door and the privy (at that time) was an open trench at the bottom of the long garden. When my father took over the tenancy the rent was two-and-sixpence a week, including rates. Later, when gas was installed, the rent was increased to four shillings – a quarter of my father's weekly wage.

Now that the house had a gas supply, the kitchen received not only a new gas-lamp but also a black gas-stove, which stood next to the old kitchen-range. This was never taken out because it still provided us with an open fire and my mother much preferred to cook on it rather than use the explosive monster from the gas-works.

During my worst illnesses my cot was brought down to our small front room so that I could be near a fire. This also made life easier for mother who did not have to climb the stairs every time I called for her. I preferred this arrangement too. Not only was the front room warmer, it was less lonely. I could hear what the daily callers were saying as they talked at our back door, and no one appeared to be in a hurry. I knew when Dora the milk-girl arrived because I heard the rattle of cans and the slurp of milk being ladled from the churn into our enamel jug, and when Eddie the baker came I could smell the newly-made bread. I recognized the heavy footsteps of the coalman, or the whistle of the insurance agent. Aunts, uncles, cousins, grandfather and grandmother, all put in an appearance at some time of the week. Sometimes they spoke in whispers, as if everything was a secret. Sometimes they wanted the whole world to hear. I learned all about the wicked girls of the town and the disgusting men who played 'gooseberry' in The Bower, a favourite 'lovers' walk' by the river. I eavesdropped on the most intimate gossip of the kitchen. The scandalous things seen in Finkle Lane, or down Mill Road, made my innocent mind burn with curiosity. A man who pretended to be a Methodist was seen coming out of The Black Swan public house, and Mrs Somebody's daughter (who'd been to grammar school and should have known better) met young men in a disused mill on the edge of town *and* took money for it ...

I had never seen any of these places but they were as lurid as sin and as gaudy as hell, and I couldn't wait to get better. Whoever would have thought such godless deeds could have been perpetrated in our little town?

What I did not hear from the kitchen or back door I overheard from the street. We had no front garden and stepped straight from our front room on to the pavement – at least we would have done if we could have used the front door. But, as that was the only corner of the room where we could put the piano (which father had bought at an auction sale), we were restricted to one entrance and exit – the back door. Nevertheless, people frequently stopped outside our window and talked for hours, so I missed very little. Local newspapers were quite unnecessary and, by the time the town-crier came round ringing his bell and bawling his declarations, the printed word was as ancient as Egyptian papyrus.

The introduction of gas into our lives now brought a new caller to the house – the gasman, who came to read and empty the meter under the stairs. He had himself been gassed in the First World War and his face was still disfigured from the burns he'd received as a soldier. He wore dark glasses, which added mystery to his puffed and purple cheeks. I'd never seen anyone wounded by war before and flinched from the imagined pain that caused such scars. But, after a few visits, I grew to know him as a kind, gentle person who invited me to go down to his gas-works as soon as I was better, or when I next had an attack of whooping-cough. Fumes from the gas-works were considered a certain cure for that complaint and were much preferred to the other alternative of swallowing a roasted mouse.

Our small front room was as crowded as the bedroom. As well as my cot and the piano, there was a large round table with six high-backed chairs, a sideboard, bookcase, accumulator-wireless, and two fireside chairs. An oval mirror hung over the mantelshelf with its two china dogs, a pendulum clock ticked on the wall above my head, and two large pictures of Scottish glens filled up the spaces left on the other walls.

The wall-clock now belongs to my youngest brother Trevor and each time I hear it chime my mind goes back more than fifty years to a night when something extraordinary happened. I must have been ill for my mother sat up with me all night long, quietly humming, worrying, praying, forcing herself to keep awake. I saw her in the firelight for a few moments, then she seemed to fade away, or rather, I felt myself fading, becoming disembodied, drifting out of time until I left my body and hovered above the bed. I saw myself perfectly still on the damp sheets below, and my mother now sobbing. Then suddenly I was no longer afraid. I experienced a radiant happiness and could not understand why I had not explored these higher regions sooner. There was no darkness, no shadows, no pain, or fading gas-lamps. And, almost immediately, I slipped back into my body and woke to see my mother winding the clock above my bed, which had either stopped, or had been stopped, and now could be started again because I was alive. The fever had passed.

A few days later I was moved back to the bedroom upstairs and left to spend much more time alone with the poker-work texts and the cracks in the ceilings. Sometimes mother would take from the blanket-chest a collection of small silk embroidered flags which were issued during the First World War. I loved their texture and bright colours as she spread them over the eiderdown. But, if they failed to interest me, she would go downstairs to the bookcase and get *An Illustrated History of the World* and bring that up for me. The large sepia pictures revealed grotesque natives with bones through their noses, or ladies with elongated necks encased in numerous rings. They were mostly naked and intrigued me. Where did they live and why were they different? Mother's answers may have been adequate at the time but those illustrations haunted me for years.

When those distractions no longer amused me, and mother had returned to her jobs in the kitchen, I lay staring at the window or trying to see how many faces I could find in the patterns on the curtains. There was little to see from the window which looked out on the street. It faced west and, in winter, I seldom saw the sun. Summer never quite made it into that room either and seemed to belong to another country beyond the glass. The nearest I came to that outside world was when the swallows, martins and swifts returned to nest under the tiles just above the window. They employed their long days racing up and down the street, halting briefly like spent arrows under the roof. The swifts were perpetually noisy with their screeching and when my grandfather said one day, 'those blessed birds need oiling' I thought he meant it. They were among the last sounds of the day, survived only by the neighbours who sat outside quietly chatting away until it was dark and their houses cool enough for sleep.

The shoe-box contains no photographs of them but I remember how their voices drawled into the fringe of twilight. The men sat on stools or broken chairs – nightwatchmen waiting for the fires of their own tiredness to burn out. Many of them, like my father, worked in the brickyards and treasured those last cooling hours of the day. The women often joined them and stood with their arms folded, adding their own small-talk to the timeless chant of the street. Sometimes a horse and cart rumbled by with its last load of hay or peas, the horseman singing incoherently to himself, his tiredness dulled by an extra pint of ale at The Boat, The Duke's Head, The White Horse or the last of the home-brewed beer he had taken to work with him. Later, towards darkness, there would occasionally be the sound of someone really drunk, staggering home and unable to find the right door, his search accompanied by an obscene soliloquy which the street took for granted, and forgave. One man, not noted for his chapel-going or religious convictions, always sang 'When the roll is called up yonder I'll be there ...'

And slowly the town sang itself to sleep, knowing that the same rituals would be gone through each day until the season changed. My parents came up to bed and once again we were all huddled together in the warm room, like a batch of bread waiting for the morning to deliver us.

2   Fold and double-fold, don't let go

Our street was just an ordinary street, or so I thought. Long and narrow, perfect for playing marbles or cowboys. You could have blocked up both ends of it and we would have survived a siege. It had everything – two grocers, two butchers, a sweet-shop, rag-and-bone man, fish-and-chips, coalman, cobbler, potato merchant, veterinary surgeon and vicar. There were five pubs, a Methodist Chapel, The Salvation Army, St Andrew's Church, and the front room of the fish-and-chip shop was used once a month by the local Roman Catholics. Every human need was provided for and everybody knew everybody else.

Many of the houses were, like ours, two-up and two-down, with long back gardens and open gateways shared by several families. There were larger houses which were privately owned but these belonged to the trades-people or gentry who lived at the posh end of the street. It was a strange mixture of the under-privileged and better-off rubbing shoulders with each other quite amicably. Every morning you would see the women sweeping that section of the pavement outside their own houses and scrubbing the steps. 'It costs nothing to keep clean or proud', said my mother, when she was asked why she bothered.

Of the many people who called at the house, I think Mr Ashby the grocer was among my favourites. His shop was only six houses away but he always delivered my mother's weekly shopping to the house. 'It's all part of the service' he would say. We only went to the shop to order, or if something was forgotten. I must have said something out of place one morning, or might have taken an item from his basket before he had ticked it on the list, for my mother scolded me. Like most grown-ups she believed that children should be seen and not heard.

'Leave him alone', said Mr Ashby, 'we were all young once.'

I found it difficult to think of him, or any other adult, as ever being young. I assumed that they were all born like that, already old.

One morning, when I did not say anything, he said, 'Where's your tongue, boy? Swallowed it?' I stuck it out, as long as my father's razor-strop, and even my mother laughed. It's just not the same fetching the groceries from the superstore.

By the time I was five I was sharing the tiny back bedroom with my sister, Freda and a new baby brother John took over my cot. The back room had a sloping ceiling and a small, swivel window. But from that window I could look out over the roof-tops of the town and imagine myself free. When the fairs came to the market-place I could see the hazy glow of orange and pink burnishing the dark sky and hear the noise of the amusements – the hurdy-gurdy music, the laughter and screams of the people enjoying themselves, and the clanging of bells. Somewhere in that gaudy underworld of naphtha flares and fortune-telling was the smell of newly made rock, candy floss and toffee-apples. Swing boats took you to the stars and dodgem cars crashed through the bounds of reality.

It was from that window that I looked out one night and saw our fowl-house on fire. I was woken by the sound of banging on the back door and whispered to my sister, 'there's someone trying to get in.'

'Yes, I know.'

'What shall we do?'

The knocking persisted until we recognized the voice of a neighbour calling below. Immediately our fears evaporated and we rushed to the window to see what was wrong. At the bottom of the garden, rays of amber light trembled into the dark and we could hear the crackling of wood under the flames. Beyond the smoke was the frantic clucking of hens and the high-pitched squeaking of the chicks which my father had reared a few days before. I rushed into my parents' bedroom, shouting, 'They're all dying! The chickens are all dying.'

For a moment I think my father thought this was no more than one of my nightmares, but as soon as he appreciated the seriousness of the alarm he quickly pulled on his trousers and rushed downstairs.

I wanted to go with him but mother kept me in the house. We watched from the kitchen window as he and some of the neighbours raced down the garden path with buckets of water. As each pail was thrown on to the fire a cloud of smoke hissed into the air and the wind carried the smell into the house. The cage of burning wood throbbed like a red-hot brand on the sky. Buckets clanked, hatchets chopped, and the men scurried backwards and forwards with more water, oblivious of the noise they made at such a late hour.

With all my fear and grief I still felt a strange kind of excitement. They were my chickens that were burning. Tomorrow I would be able to tell the world of this drama. It happened to me. None of the other boys in our street – Eric, Sid, Francis, Dennis, Alan and Keith – had ever known anything like this. It was an unparalleled tragedy, and it was mine.

In the morning when I went down to view the scene of desolation, there were only a few charred timbers and a heap of black, twisted wire-netting left. A cluster of scorched feathers still stuck to the wall. Some little bones lay scattered on the floor. When I looked into the dustbin I found the blistered shell of the old night-heater which had caused the fire. Somehow it had been knocked over and set light to the straw. We never rebuilt the fowl-house. That corner of the garden became an extra square of playground, a neglected wilderness that was eventually taken over by wild horseradish, thistles, squabbling sparrows, and butterflies. Of all the pets we had once owned, only the rabbits remained. The pigeons had gone, the cat disappeared, the chickens were dead. Noah's Ark was vacant.

The rest of the garden was taken up with growing vegetables. The rows took on the same pattern each year – carrots, parsnips, broad-beans, onions, potatoes, marrows and leeks, the order never varied. One of my first jobs was to use my toy-hoe to help keep down the weeds, for which I earned twopence. Another was collecting butterflies and caterpillars off the cabbages. For this I had a jamjar with a paper lid and if I caught more than twenty in one day I got another twopence.

The only other building at the bottom of the garden was the wash-house. This was a broken-down shed of many-coloured bricks and ill-fitting tiles through which you could see the sky. It felt as ancient as a pyramid and served several purposes as well as being just a wash-house. It was where we kept the coal, where father chopped the kindling for our fires and kept his bicycle. And it was where (before the disastrous fire) grandfather plucked the latest victim from the fowl-house to provide us with our Sunday dinner.

One of the jobs I did not like as I grew older was helping father chop the wood. He would sit down on a sack and split the logs with a sharp hatchet, leaving me to pick up the kindling to fill the other sacks. With two fires to keep going in the house each day, and the fires for the copper, we needed a lot of wood to see us through the week. By the time we had finished this task I was cold, dirty and thoroughly miserable.

The copper in the corner of the wash-house was used twice a week – for Monday morning wash-day and for boiling the water on Saturday nights for our weekly bath. There were a few other occasions when it was brought into service, like boiling the Christmas puddings or a large ham, and I once hid in it after getting into trouble.

Wash-day was always Monday, wet or fine. Then the crumbling building puffed with steam and smelt of carbolic soap. 'Nip up to the house and get me a blue-bag', mother would ask as she cleaned the washing-line that stretched the whole length of the garden. Soon the copper was boiling, the sheets frothing and foaming as if alive, the shirts regaining their natural colours, and our underwear being made decent for public display. Then the scrubbing-board and the dolly-tub came into use and the wicker basket began piling up with all the garments which had been hung out to dry. Pillow-cases billowed out like fat uncles, pyjamas played acrobats as the clothes' prop lifted the washing-line even higher into the air, and neighbours cast a competitive eye along each garden to see whose wash looked whitest. When the sheets were dry I helped mother to fold them ready for ironing. 'You take your end, I'll take mine', she said, almost as a chant, 'fold and double-fold ... don't let go.'

The phrase returns to me now with the same magic of 'Ride a cock-horse to Banbury Cross ...'

Just a few weeks before my mother died in her eighty-fifth year, we sat holding hands and talking about those distant days when we spent so much time in each other's company –

> Our two hands had not touched like that
> since fifty years ago I helped her fold
> the white sheets from the washing-line.
> Starting apart we shook each one
> from head to foot, from left to right,
> until it shortened and our hands
> met like the hands of those who meet
> in stately order at a dance.
>
> *You take your end, I'll take mine,*
> *fold and double-fold, don't let go ...*
> It was a ritual that made
> each Monday morning Reckitts-blue
> and taught me innocently of love.
> Now she lies white with hands that will
> not tug or pull at sheets again,
> or shorten longer distances.
>
> With her late death a childhood dies
> and there's no point in asking questions now.
> Nor can my words begin to tell
> this double grief I feel. The path
> where once we stood and laughed
> is gone. But somewhere I still hear
> *You take your end, I'll take mine,*
> *fold and double-fold, don't let go ...*

If Monday was always wash-day, Saturday was always bath night. The water which had been boiled in the copper was carried in pails up to the house where a long zinc bath stood in the kitchen, like a ship in dry dock, waiting to receive both water and child. The hot water was cooled with rain-water from the corrugated water-tank outside the back door, then in I went, to be wrung out a few minutes later, white and laundered for another week. Then it was my sister's turn and, finally, my parents. When everyone had finished, the old zinc battleship was hung once more on the wall outside until next Saturday night came round and a new fire was lit under the copper. From the small window of my bedroom I watched the smoke fade from the wash-house chimney and the first faint stars appear over the roof tops of the houses in Broad Street, and beyond them the tall spire of St Mary's Church faded into the darkening sky.

Downstairs, the wireless went through its own Saturday ritual of *In Town Tonight, Variety Music Hall, Appointment with Fear, Henry Hall's Guest Night, Victor Sylvester's Ballroom Dancing,* and *Vic Oliver.* The kitchen was then restored to one of its many functions as my parents started preparing for our Sunday dinner. Father would roast the joint while mother baked tarts and a sponge cake.

The kitchen was a funny little room, covered with blue linoleum and a home-made pegged rug in front of the fireplace. On either side of the kitchen-range were cupboards and at night, when it was quiet, with only the hiss of the gas-mantle, you could hear crickets clicking from the dark shelves, or mice nibbling down below. The cupboards on the right-hand side of the fire were removed to make way for the gas-cooker but I think the live stock simply moved to the other side and took up residence there, for the sounds were just as noticeable, perhaps even more so, and I listened nervously to all their activities. And then the snap of a trap, and I knew that one mouse had met its end. We set traps in the cupboard under the stairs too, where the gas-meter ticked and the home-made wine was kept, and I would wince at the crack of the spring when another mouse was caught.

The kitchen was where my father also did our shoe repairs. He had his own cobbler's last and bought his leather from the shoe-repairer in our street. I watched him many times as he cut a piece of leather down to size and put a dozen sprigs between his lips, just like a proper cobbler, then nailed the new sole neatly on to an old shoe. 'You needn't think you'll get a new pair', he'd say, 'until you've learnt to look after these.' My brother looked on ruefully, knowing that when I had outgrown these boots they would be handed down to him. 'These toe-caps need some polish' father said, in a tone which I knew meant 'do something about it!' He pulled the boot from the last and handed it to me. 'There you are. I've put some extra blakeys in the heels and, with a bit of luck, they'll see you through until the spring.' I thanked him sadly and wore the boots until the winter snow ate through the perished uppers and he had no option then but to throw them on the fire and say to mother. 'You'd better take him over to Miss Mann's shoe-shop in the morning to get a new pair, and make sure they're big enough to last!'

Were they the boots that had once come out of the shoe-box that now held the photographs? Perhaps not. There were to be several shoe-boxes to come from Miss Mann's shop, which had wooden steps and a thatched roof. I remember going into it with my mother to buy my new shoes and thinking that all the shelves looked full of small coffins. Miss Mann, like all good shopkeepers in those days, treated her customers as royalty. She was a well-spoken, slightly fussy lady who took endless trouble over getting the right fit of shoe for whichever pair of feet she had in front of her. Her shop, like so many I knew as a child, has long since disappeared to make way for a busy road that takes the traffic through the town. With its demolition went a lot of the old-fashioned courtesies.

I return to the shoe-box with its photographs and wonder why some of them appear not to have anything to do with our family. Why, for instance, is there a photograph of the funeral of the first young man in our town to be killed in the First World War? Why, for that matter, was he brought home for burial instead of being buried in Flanders with all the other millions of his generation? I turn the photograph over to look on the back. There is a pencil note saying that the second bearer on the left is my grandfather, who made officiating at other people's funerals something of a vocation. It kept him in 'baccy' or gave him another 'churchwarden pipe' to add to his collection. Because he was a tall, strong man he was often in demand as a coffin-bearer and told many amusing, but sad stories about those events; none more pathetic than when it was the funeral of a pauper, paid for by the parish. The cheap, crudely made coffin was not very substantial and sometimes the corpse slipped out from the bottom as the box was lowered down from a small bedroom window because they couldn't get it down the stairs. 'Back up you git, Cyril. You'll meet Old Nick soon enough!' he'd say, and we would all laugh.

When I was ill, it was grandfather who frequently walked up to the doctor's surgery to collect the latest box of pills or bottle of medicine prescribed for me. When he returned he would sit by my bedside and talk about the fields where he worked and of the animals he had known in the fens. He brought the smell of the fens with him into my room. I could tell the seasons of the year by the smells on his jacket – hay, corn, potatoes, celery, horses. I looked forward to his visits. Sometimes, out of one of his large pockets, he would produce a newly laid egg for my tea, or an apple which he had polished until it looked like marble. Then he would split it in half with his big thumbs and share it with me. He was also my chief medicine-taster and, whatever potion he brought back from the doctor's surgery, it had to have his approval first. Putting the bottle to his lips he pretended to drink a quarter of the contents and then said, 'My goodness, boy! That's a right drop of good stuff he's given you this time. If that don't make you better I don't know what will.' I respected his judgement and took my medicine, not questioning why the bottle was always still full when he put it back on my bedside table.

I can hardly recognize him from this photograph of the soldier's funeral, but there is another one of him sitting with grandmother outside our back door. She is wearing a long black dress with an embroidered bodice, large brooch and a necklace. He sits uncomfortably in his Sunday suit, collar and tie, eyeing the photographer suspiciously and eager for the formalities to be over.

When my mother was in hospital just before she died I met an old man in the same geriatric ward who said to me, 'You're one of John Henry's boys, 'nt you?'

'Slip a generation', I replied, 'and you'd be getting close.'

'I worked with 'im when I were young. One of the best thackers I ever knew. At 'arvest time he'd bind more wheat in a day than three of us ... And you're his son?'

'No', I explained again. 'My father was.'

He chuckles. 'Allus up to summat, he was. Played more tricks on me than trees have crows. God knows where 'e got 'is ideas from. He'd come roaring down the drove on 'is old bike, singing 'is 'ead off. Thin as a bloody rake.'

I tried to imagine grandfather as a young man, working in

the fields I have known and taken for granted all these years. Although he had worked in the gravel-pits and the brickyards he had spent most of his working life on the land. He would have known days like this, when clouds hammer the fens as though earth itself were an anvil – himself a maker of moods.

'You're just like 'im' the old man said again. 'Knew by your eyes the minute you walked in ... That's one of John Henry's boys, I said to meself. Same quirky stare and turn of the head. Full of mischief.'

I did not try to correct him again but asked if he could remember anything else about him.

'Not a lot. If he didn't want your hoss to work it bloody well wouldn't. He'd rub a dead mackerel round the manger and you couldn't get that hoss out of the stall arter that. I were only a boy then. We worked on Wheatley's farm at the time.'

'But why would he want to stop anyone's horse from working?'

'To teach some bugger a lesson more often than not. There were some lazy, mischievous devils about even then. I remember one old boy hid John Henry's bike up a tree so he couldn't git home for an hour. 'E got 'is own back next morning.'

The old man's face lit up when the deeds of ninety years ago shone through the winters of the room where he sat. At least my grandfather did not spend his dark days strapped in a chair among the sad, frail, spoon-fed patients of that ward. At seventy-four he pegged the ridge of his last stack and said, 'That's it! I've done my whack.' He died three years later on 4 September 1944.

He was an immensely lovable, kind, humorous man in his quiet way, a man to look up to. I remember his eyes, tender and steady, his hands gentle but strong. A calm man, not easily influenced by others. In his younger days he liked to go for long walks in the evenings by himself, but he always said to his wife (who liked to go to bed early). 'leave the light burning in the window until I get home.' He never locked his house. 'It'd take two people to rob me,' he'd often say, 'one to bring it and the other to take it away.'

To me, as an impressionable child, there was nothing he did not know about the world of farming – ploughing, sowing, claying, hayricks and harvesting. He had started work on the land at the age of seven, tending sheep for fourpence a day, working for most of the farmers in the area, even when it meant walking or cycling eight miles each morning to make sure of keeping his job. He knew how to cure cows when blood got into their milk and what to do for horses when they were sick, and he was, as the old man in the hospital said, the best builder of straw-stacks for miles around.

When there were no jobs to be found on the land he took 'piece-work' in the gravel-pits or knot-holes of the local brickyards. In those days there were no mechanical shalers or excavators to get the blue clay to the surface. It was all done by hand, by crow-bar, pick and shovel, trolleys and wheelbarrows; manual labour with a vengeance. Once, he discovered the fossil of a 500-million-year-old fish preserved in the clay and knew that it must be of some importance. So he reported it to the foreman of the yard, who in turn contacted the curator of Peterborough Museum, who then got in touch with a scientist at Cambridge University and, eventually, the fossil found its way to the Natural History Museum in London. As a reward grandad and his work-mates were given a free meal at The Bull Hotel in Peterborough. Next morning they returned to their more normal labours of making bricks and eating their modest 'dockey' in the pits. Since then many similar fossils have been found, including the skeleton of a plesiosaur that existed here a mere 160 million years ago.

Grandfather had also known a period of working as a coalman in London, selling coal to the impoverished East-enders by the lump instead of by the sack. But the smog and damp of the city, as well as the twelve-hour days of coal-carting, affected his health and the doctor advised him to return to the cleaner air of the fens. As four of my grandparents' children had already died in London, it was advice that both were willing to accept. If the rest of the family was to survive, there was only one place to be – home. And, for them, home was the small but independent town of Whittlesey in the Isle of Ely.

It was just as well for, if there is any kind of destiny, then my own beginnings in the fens were made possible by that

return and my father, who was born on 22 May 1902, was
later to start the next generation of Storeys. So my sense of
'belonging' is, I feel, deeper than just my own life. I am sure
there is not only continuity in our existence but an
overlapping of time, so that the beginnings and the ends
of it are outside our individual life-span. The town itself was
a perpetuation of several layers of history interlocking in the
slow progress from one age to another.

History has a way of kicking up a few stones to reveal what
was there before – customs hidden beneath the artifices of
other times, facts that are left behind in unlikely places like
initials cut into the bark of an old tree.

I was thinking about the town's past only a few months
ago when I received a surprise telephone call from a
gentleman who had bought a second-hand sideboard and
found in one of its drawers a hand-made notebook belonging
to a James Spencer. Spencer was a solicitor's clerk in
Whittlesey who died in 1827 at the age of twenty. He was a
promising young poet and would have become a splendid
local historian had his life been longer. As it was he left
several notebooks (usually made out of old bills of sale) and
in them recorded many details of the town's history.

> *1291.* In Pope Nicholas's Taxation the Vicarage of
> Whittlesey St Andrew is valued at £3.6.8d and the Rectory
> at £10. By 1535 the value of the vicarage was raised to
> £4.13.4d ... In 1603 the Rectory was sold.

Page after page of dates and statutes passed through the
reigns of English kings and queens, reminding me that while
great national events were taking place elsewhere, life was
making its own history in our local parish where the
arguments over tithes and grazing rights were as bitter as
anything seen in present-day trade agreements or the
community charge.

If I stood and listened there were echoes in the street, in the
stone houses and brick cottages, in the lanes and fields. Some
tithes were never paid 'by reason they could not distinguish
what parish they lay in – St Andrew's or St Mary's.' We lived
in St Andrew's and were loyal to any of its claims even
though my family had little time for the Church. Often those

claims went far beyond the parish boundaries for 'the Manor and Rectory of St Mary have always been considered to belong to the Abbey of Thorney whereas the Manor, Rectory or Parsonage of St Andrew have always been considered to belong to the Priory of Ely.'

History? How much are we aware of its influence in the shaping of our lives when we are only children, or adults for that matter? Until I read James Spencer's notebook I knew nothing of the Isle of Ely Militia which:

'On 8th May 1716 issued an Order to the Township of Whittlesey to Furnish 24 foot-soldiers and 7 horse-soldiers.' But Whittlesey people aren't bossed around that easily and the inhabitants objected to the Deputy Lieutenants of the County who made a land re-assessment and reduced the quota to 4 foot-soldiers and 1 horse-soldier, 'every soldier to be provided with a musket four-feet long in barrel, a bayonet, cartridge-box and sword.'

One entry which I found especially interesting was an extract from a document about the town's markets and fairs:

King George the First in the 2nd year of his reign, on the application of George Downs, Gentlemen of the Inner Temple, London, Granted to the said G. Downs on behalf of the several inhabitants of Whittlesey, by Letters Patent under the Great Seal of Great Britain, dated 17th February 1715, a Market on Friday *forever* for all wares and Merchandize, and Also three Fairs, to wit, on the 11th June, 25th October, and 25th January in every year for all Cattle, Goods, Wares and Merchandize whatever ... Each Fair to last 3 days.

How easy it is to take the markets and fairs of today for granted, to forget the arguments, debates, applications and resolutions that made the town what it is now. I am, I hope, sufficiently grateful that my grandfather was advised by his London doctor to return to the cleaner air of the fens. Had he not done so I might not have been born and certainly would not have been writing this book.

Coincidence? Accident? What determines our place in history? James Spencer's notebook also contained an extract from the Records of Assessment in 1770 which showed that our family existed in Whittlesey then under the name of John

Household Storey. But I believe we can go back much further than that. Our surname is a derivation of the Scottish, maybe Scandinavian, name Storrie, meaning strong. It is possible that it was introduced into the fens during the seventeenth-century when Scottish prisoners-of-war were brought down from Dunbar to help Sir Cornelius Vermuyden drain the area.

Had James Spencer lived a few more years he would have been able to record the epidemic of cholera which struck Whittlesey in 1832 or the triumphs of another local man – Sir Harry Smith who became known as the Hero of Aliwal after serving under Clive of India in 1846.

The history of Whittlesey of course goes back to unrecorded time and several of our street names have their origins in earlier occupations – Roman, Saxon, Danish and Dutch. But, even earlier are those tribes we so far know little about. Recent excavations at Flag Fen have revealed what an important and commercial region this was for Bronze Age people, and how organized they were. Who knows what revelations will turn up in some other piece of second-hand furniture or forgotten cupboard. What is history but a 'whodunit' written by many hands.

And so my story continues in the place where it belongs.

3   The price of stolen rhubarb

The doctor who attended my birth – Dr Andrew Bernard – was to influence me in several ways long after he had ceased caring for me as one of his patients. But when I was a child the words I longed to hear him speak were, 'I think, Mrs Storey, that this young man is well enough now to sit out in the garden, or better still go for a walk into the fens.' Though, when I think about it, any words spoken by our family doctor were music to my ears for he was a most gentle, serene man with a quiet, beautiful voice that made a lasting impression upon me. He pronounced words with such care that I believed them to be extremely valuable. His pronunciation was clear and precise, with sonorously prolonged vowels and slightly emphasized consonants. To me he was a rare, unearthly figure in our coarser world and when I asked my mother why he sounded so different from us she said, 'It's because he's a doctor.'

Half a century later, when I met him again in his native Scotland, I knew it was not just because he was a doctor. He loved language and, at the age of eighty-four, still used it with the same reverence and precision I remembered as a child. To my surprise he could recall the night of my birth, as if it was no more than a few years ago. He was, he told me, just coming to the end of a lecture on Emily Brontë at the local literary society, when he was informed that my mother was in labour. 'Maternity work was a fate of mine and I have to admit that my passion was literature and my profession medicine', he said with a smile. 'I thought you would not mind waiting a few minutes longer.'

Dr Bernard had arrived in Whittlesey as a young man in need of some experience before moving on to what he believed would be the more lucrative south. 'I said once upon a time to everyone here – when I qualify I shall go down to the fen country for about three months. I do want to see the fens of England.' As it was, he stayed for more than thirty years and left the town as quietly as he had arrived. 'Is that news good or bad? I thought that as I came without any fuss I wanted to leave without any fuss. I thought I had served my apprenticeship fairly well, my visit had worked out satisfactorily and I needed a change. So I departed unobtrusively and refused any organized goodbye. Besides, I could not have borne it emotionally.'

After his retirement he was able to satisfy another passion – travel, and I was to receive several long letters from him when he was visiting some of his favourite places – Vienna, Italy, India and especially Bali, 'with the best sunsets in the world'. For many years he had wanted to go to Czechoslovakia but was very disappointed and wrote – 'Give me the Tuscan skies and the warm south – or, as Browning confessed 'Ope my heart and you will see / Graved inside of it – *Italy!*' – and he knew.'

Our correspondence began in 1971, shortly after the publication of my book *Portrait of the Fen Country*, which had been sent to him by an old friend. It was only then that I learned of his deep love of English literature:

> I am so glad you brought John Clare into your book – a poet I have always valued & loved – I had read him when I took Arts before Medicine at Glasgow University; he was among 'The Nature Poets', Burns, James Hogg & The others ... And it was one of my first jaunts when I went to live in Whittlesey, viz – a pilgrimage to the Clare country where on several afternoons I walked, solitary, on those roads about Helpstone where *he* had walked. I still look up his poems with their moving beauty ...

The two American poets he liked most were Emily Dickinson and Robert Frost but, he said, 'Life allows me little time to indulge in twentieth-century poetry, which may account for my thin approach to the 'modern poets' you mention.' He had expressed the opinion that 'All the old virtues, skills and craft have gone from the poets of today. There is no discipline or eloquence among them any more.' I suggested he would find both in the poems of W.H.Auden and Dylan Thomas, to which he replied:

> I am sure it is my own lack of understanding but I find the first of those two gentlemen too superficial and the second too obscure. I shall always remain in allegiance to those earlier masters – Shelley, Byron and Keats (is there another poem in the language to breathe more pure air than the *Ode to a Nightingale?* ...

He was then very generous in his remarks about a volume of my own poems which he had recently bought in Glasgow:

> They have all given me great, sober pleasure. You write with such sincerity and love for the land, the winds that blow over the fens, and the people of the earth – especially your grandfather. I remember him well, and your grandmother. I saw a great deal of them and, of course, your mother and father. Do remember me to them with the kindest of memories ... I hear that Whittlesey is being pulled down and flung about and stretched and put together again. The old place didn't seem too bad when I was there ...

As much as he loved poetry I am sure that his greatest delight came from good prose writers. In writing to me on my birthday in February 1976 he said:

> I have just enjoyed immensely rereading E.M.Forster's *Passage to India*. What a delight. So rare in thought and expression ... I found similar joys in Katharine Mansfield's lovely *Journal* and her *Letters*. I went one afternoon in London to look across a street in St John's Wood, at the house where she wrote of the death of her brother ... I also went to her grave in Fontain-bleau – a flat stone with Shakesperian quotation ... And I walked along one afternoon beside a crying, restless sea at Menton on the French Riveria, to stand outside the house where she wrote so many of her fine stories and letters – a house, taken over by the French literary people in memory of her, for it was the French who first recognized her genius ... I have just read for the nth time her wonderful *Je Ne Parle Pas Français* and urge you to do so if you are not already acquainted with it ...

Although we now corresponded we did not actually meet again, since his departure from Whittlesey thirty years earlier, until we met in a Glasgow hotel on the eve of my departure for a holiday on the Isle of Arran. He had wanted me to stay with him but he was not living at home at the time – 'I'm looking after some dear old friends nearby who are not at all well.' My train was an hour late and I was fearing that he might have given up and left. But he was still there with a huge box of chocolates, the same neatly dressed man without a line on his face and looking almost the same as he did the last time I saw him in his surgery at Whittlesey. We talked most of the time about literature and, referring to my birth-night, he said 'I always felt gratified to learn years later that the child who disturbed my talk on Emily Brontë should turn out to be a writer.' He stared at me seriously, as though he were about to prepare me for an unwelcome diagnosis. 'You do admire the Brontës, I trust?' We moved from the Brontës to Jane Austen and then to Rose Macaulay. 'I always wish' he said, 'that I had written to tell her of my gratitude for her wit, fun, fine prose and wisdom. But I never had the nerve.'

The evening came to an end and he invited me to go and stay with him in the spring, when he hoped to be back in his own home. That was not to be. Four days later he died, a loss I was not to know about until I returned from my holiday and my parents showed me the news in the local paper. I realized then with sorrow what an important friendship I had missed and how fortunate I had been to have a doctor like him. I would have written to him sooner, if I'd had the nerve.

If, for some reason, Dr Bernard could not come to our house when a doctor was needed, his partner – Dr Lawson – took his place. I did not care for him as much and do not remember him as clearly. He spoke with an impatient, clipped delivery and his calls were always brief. He often did his rounds on horseback, galloping right up to our kitchen door before dismounting. Then he rushed into the house, carried out his examination and, within seconds, was gone. As the sound of the horse's hooves faded beyond the gate, mother would say 'That man's more like a blessed whirlwind than a doctor. You'd think he was robbing a bank instead of visiting the sick.'

My parents must have wished frequently that neither doctor had to attend to us too often. It was not easy for them in the thirties to meet doctors' bills and all our medical expenses had to be paid for then out of the small wages my father earned in the brickyards. During the Depression this did not even guarantee regular work. It was sometimes one week at work and one week on the dole. There were many times when my parents went without meat so that their children could be cared for. If a chicken disappeared from the fowl-run, or a rabbit was taken from its hutch, we soon knew why. Nor was I so conscience-stricken that when the rabbit-skin was given to me to take to the rag-and-bone man, I did not hesitate to dash off to claim the two or three pence I knew I would get for it, a profit which was quickly spent at the corner sweet-shop on liquorice bootlaces or aniseed balls.

Although our house was small, the large garden provided us with plenty of vegetables and, with a plateful of Norfolk dumplings (which grandmother called 'sinkers') and some Bisto gravy, our hunger was assuaged. Our friendly grocer, Mr Ashby, also slipped a bunch of bananas into my mother's shopping from time to time without putting them on the bill. Looking at some of those early photographs taken of me during those years I can see I was far too chubby to have gone without for long. I was to spend many hours in that garden, enjoying my own company and making up games in which I played all the roles. Although I don't think I had a great deal of courage I did enjoy climbing on to the roof of the wash-house and the chicken-run, from which I would then jump with a feeling of exhilaration, hoping that the neighbours would see what a dare-devil I was. One of the pleasures of getting on to the roof was to see over the wall into the garden on the other side. This belonged to a school-teacher, of whom quite a few of the children in our street were afraid, and we used to despair if our ball went over into her garden, which was full of flowers and bushes. Rather than risk her wrath by going round to her house in Whitmore Street to ask for it back, we would climb over the wall and hope not to be seen.

But these adventures were to come later. I did not become so daring until I started school. Before then my games were more solitary and my acquaintance with the rest of the town only came when the doctor told my mother that she could now take me out for some fresh air. The summer excursions are the ones I remember most. We would set off down the street, passing the fish-and-chip shop, the cobbler's, the Methodist chapel, The White Horse, the Salvation Army, the two butchers' shops, the coal merchant and vicarage. Now I knew where Mr Blake and Mr Whitehead lived, where Turner's and Winterton's shops were. We passed St Andrew's church and *The Letter B* public house and, by the time we reached Briggate Bridge, we had to decide whether to continue down Ramsey Road, or turn right to Black Bush and a walk by the river. Whichever way we took delighted me for I was now liberated into a world of space and sky that was to excite me for the rest of my life. Fields shimmered in the hot afternoon sun and the sky was the colour of cornflowers.

As a child I did not understand the nature of our local geography. I had no idea why the earth was so flat, so vast and so compellingly vibrant with light, and so quiet. I assumed the whole world was like that and took those immense skies and distances for granted. We picked dandelions for the rabbits, wild flowers for the kitchen window-sill, and blackberries for a pie. The countryside offered so much. Around me were skylarks, kingfishers, the occasional heron, pheasants, hares, bulrushes, poppies and buttercups, and, on the western horizon, the slender brickyard chimneys squeezing their perpetual smoke into the translucent air. Along the river-bank were yellow flag-irises, bushes of hawthorn and wild rose – colours and smells as indelible as birthmarks.

If our walk took us down Ramsey Road it was not long before we came to the railway-crossing, where we stopped to talk to the gate-keeper, Bill Coles, who played in the same brass band as my father. While he and mother talked I listened to the chirping conversation of the bells in his wooden hut. These told of the next train's approach, sometimes one from each direction. Long before the train came into view I heard its wheels singing along the tracks. Then the first puffs of smoke rose from above the workers' allotments and the engine appeared from round a cluster of nearby bushes. Mr Coles checked his watch, waved to the driver, changed the signals and returned to his hut to await another bell. I stood and looked at the carriages as they passed, thinking how wonderful it must be to travel such long distances by train – to March, Ely, Norwich ... and so fast.

When the gates were reopened we continued our walk into the fens and mother showed me the fields where she and my grandfather had worked, pea-picking, potato-picking, harvesting, carrot-pulling and haymaking. I knew nothing then of the floods, drainage, riots, resentments and hunger which had made the fen country a bitter place in which to live. I knew nothing of the winters that gripped the land in a vice of frost and snow, making men idle for weeks at a time without work or money. My winters were lived mostly indoors near a coal-fire or in bed. I knew, so far, only the summers when wheat ripened to mahogany brown and tar bubbled on the road which stretched into an eternity of blue. If there were clouds they were white and majestic, piled high as ice-cream on the rim of the world. Sometimes my mother would ask me to see shapes in the clouds, just as she used to ask me to find faces in the wallpaper or bedroom curtains. 'For goodness sake, boy, use your imagination. What can you see? What do the clouds remind you of?' She had no idea that she was playing Hamlet's game and would suggest all kinds of shapes.

If we did not go towards Ramsey Road we strolled down by the river which led to Black Bush and another railway-crossing. We seldom went as far as the gates but turned instead along the river-bank where there was a small gravelled area. Here the water was shallow enough for me to paddle in and count the minnows sniffing round my feet. I could also make reed boats and send them off, racing downstream if there was a breeze. You made reed boats simply by taking a stout reed and bending the tip over to thread through the base. The spear then made a keel and the loop a spinnaker which caught the wind and took the boat off at great speed. If you were adept at this you could have a whole Armada afloat in no time.

It was along this stretch of water that I was to first try my hand at fishing, with a home-made rod, cotton-thread line and bent pin for a hook. I never caught anything but it was a pastime that enabled me to observe what else was going on – moorhens, swans, reed-buntings, and the distant caw of rooks in the trees around the church of St Andrew's. Beyond St Andrew's I could see the tall spire of St Mary's and, on those lazy afternoons, the town seemed to rock sleepily in an invisible hammock.

A little farther along the bank was a place which used to serve as the town's swimming-pool and, beyond that, was what we called 'the black bridge' which crossed the river. This was a railway-bridge and I liked to stand beneath it when a train went over. Then we continued towards the brickyards and round by fields known as Cantors' Dole and back home in time for tea.

If we went to neither Black Bush nor Ramsey Road, my mother would take me down Station Road to the recreation ground. One of the attractions of this walk was passing the blacksmith's forge, where we stopped to watch him making a horseshoe. It was all part of the day out, as essential as the bag of sherbet from the sweet-shop or a ride on the swings. I always thought he kept the shimmering ashes of his fire waiting until we reached his doorway, then, with a gush from the bellows, they would explode into a galaxy of sparks which flew into those dusty spaces where all the undone jobs still waited. The metal melted, the first straight bar shone like gold as it was lifted from the forge to the anvil, and soon the hammer was beating it into shape. It took time and skill. The shoe was reheated, beaten, dipped in a bucket of water, refired, was hammered again with a rhythm more ancient than the forge itself, and soon the shoe was finished. In the yard opposite, a horse pawed the ground, impatient to be shod. Although I did not care for the singeing smell when the hot shoe was pressed on to the hoof, I can remember my admiration for this man who could beat and fashion things like that from ore and fire.

Another attraction of going to Station Road recreation ground was to see my first girlfriend – a scraggy little creature of five who loved climbing *up* the slide and going head-first down the steps. She always had scabby knees and a runny nose and I once made her cry by telling her that she had dirty knickers. Whether this was early male chauvinism or the result of my puritanical upbringing I do not know. On another occasion I know I pushed her off the swings and later buried her in the sand-pit. Such acts of violence were soon forgotten and each week we looked forward to our meetings when we ran through the grass or got soaked through at the drinking-fountain. Who was she? I do not know. I cannot even remember her name, only her gangley-legs, mouse-like face, and limp black hair.

When these afternoons were over and we returned home, the house felt cramped and stuffy. Flies buzzed with an incessant hum, hovering in a small orbit round the lampshade until, in a moment of carelessness, they got themselves stuck on to the yellow flypaper hanging like a sticky stalactite from the ceiling. There, for a few seconds, they tried to tear their delicate wings from the glue, kicking their legs into the air until they became still. Swatting them with copies of the *Daily Herald* was, I thought, much more humane and my father was an expert at whacking them.

One of the first tasks mother had to put her mind to was the preparation of our early evening meal, which I think we just called 'tea' even though it was cooked. From the black gas-stove in the corner of the kitchen came the smell of bacon boiling and of cabbage or broad-beans cooking in the steamer. While the meat and vegetables cooked, she made a bowl of parsley sauce or prepared the 'spotted dick' for afters. Sometimes the pudding could be an apple or rhubarb pie and I liked to help myself to a piece before it disappeared under a roof of pastry. Once, when standing on a chair to reach towards the forbidden bowl, I fell and gashed my forehead on the corner of the table, which meant a quick call to the doctor for emergency repairs. The price of stolen rhubarb was more than I had bargained for and the scar remains with me to this day. But, barring accidents, our tea was finally ready and we waited for father to return from work. On hot days his shirt was rusty with sweat and brick-dust, his hands swollen and bruised from working in the kilns. After taking off his boots he asked for a drink of water. The only water-tap we had was in the yard and shared by four other families in our row. Most of the men arrived home at roughly the same time, so it frequently meant a fight between the children to see who could draw the first jug of water. There was no point in getting it sooner for the men liked it as cold as could be. While father quenched his thirst my sister cleaned-out his tea-bottle. Most of the brickyard workers believed that there was nothing better for their thirst than cold tea and they used old pop-bottles with spring caps for this and took a generous supply with them to work. We cleaned the bottles by putting small pebbles into them, half-filled with water, then shook them vigorously (as if mixing a cocktail) to descale the brown tan from the glass.

By the time father had washed and put on a clean shirt, we were sitting at table, ready for the meal to start. Someone was chosen to say grace, then mother served us in strict order of seniority. Our meals were always accompanied by a cup of tea – a beverage so strong that it was nearly chewable. It was brewed, or *mashed* as mother would say, in a big brown enamel teapot which had belonged to her grandmother. With four or five teaspoonfuls of loose tea went a generous pinch of bicarbonate-of-soda to bring out the flavour.

The one meal that did not have tea as an accompaniment was Sunday dinner. For this we had a bottle of Corona, either dandelion-and-burdock, or ginger beer. We always knew when it was Sunday in our house, not only because of the Corona, nor because we had to dress in our best clothes for Sunday School, nor because the church bells made the rooks angry in Mr Boyce's walnut trees, but because we always had a clean starched tablecloth which had to last the rest of the week. It was the day when we also had Yorkshire pudding with gravy for starters, and stewed plums with custard for afters.

Even the street looked cleaner on Sundays. People put fresh flowers in their windows or polished their aspidistras, and children normally seen in patched trousers or torn dresses now pranced about in suits or pleated skirts, whether they went to Sunday School or not. I had no choice. I was sent morning and afternoon, then went with my parents to the service in the evening. Although my parents remained loyal Congregationalists all their lives, we were, as children, moved about from Sunday School to Sunday School, sometimes to chapel, sometimes to the Salvation Army (because that's where they had more music) and then back to the 'Congs'. As our daily education at school was in the hands of the Church of England, our religious upbringing was interdenominational, if not secure.

The observance of the Lord's Day was taken very seriously.

We were not allowed to play with our toys or read our comics and the only radio programmes we had on were religious. My mother took some pride in saying that whilst bringing up her family she had never been reduced to washing nappies on Sundays. Those 'Church of England christians' who were known to do jobs on the sabbath were frowned upon by the chapel-goers who took the commandment to keep it holy as paramount in the pilgrim's progress to eternal life. All the jobs that could have been done on Sunday, like cleaning shoes, chopping sticks, cutting fingernails or cooking the Sunday joint, were performed on Saturday.

Despite these restrictions I enjoyed the day and felt free to enter my own world of make believe, especially at Sunday School where I was no longer under the eye of my parents. I learnt in that small hall where our classes were held, what it meant to be an individual. There I could say 'yes' and 'no' just as I pleased. I could sing, shout, clap, sulk, put my feet on the chairs, and no one could do anything about it. I could play with sand in a miniature Garden of Eden, saying to myself 'that's not a real serpent', or I could pull off the head of a cardboard Daniel and feel one up on the lions. I could drop pieces of rubber or orange-peel on to the top of the tortoise-stove when no one was looking and sit with angelic indifference as the rubber or peel melted, filling the hall with its own irreligious incense. It was there where I was taught to believe in a world of 'five loaves and two fishes' feeding five thousand I wondered how Mr Blake at our fish-and-chip shop would have coped with that lot.

Perhaps the only real doubt I had then was that every hair of my head was numbered, so I would deliberately pull one or two out to see if I could upset divine calculations. That some children died and went to heaven seemed acceptable, even sensible. After the funeral of one of the little girls in my class I imagined heaven to be full of children running around in celestial fields of warm grass with all the stars turned to skylarks and freckled angels playing on mouth-organs in the hedgerows, so vivid was the preacher's description of that happy land beyond the skies.

The child's funeral took place one hot afternoon in summer. The entire Sunday School walked behind her coffin as it was carried through the town. I did not know it then but the feeling was not unlike that of being part of some half-forgotten Greek tragedy. The small girl could have been a child-queen mourned by her people. The shops were closed. The streets lined with silent, weeping people. The procession moved with a calm, simple, primitive dignity, not in step but with a slow rhythmic shuffle that gave the long cortege some order. Some of the older children (my sister among them) were chosen as bearers and walked in front carrying the coffin. The child's parents followed with other members of the family, all dressed in deep mourning, their audible grief rising and fading through the afternoon like an ancient chant. Behind the family walked the Sunday School children – the girls in white dresses and the boys in white shirts – all with a small bow of black ribbon pinned to them, and all carrying a single white flower. In the dry summer sunlight the white dazzled in contrast with the black suits of the adults, and our smaller footsteps added a syncopated echo to their tread. The church bell was tolling, the rooks cawing. People stood on the edge of the pavements, watching the procession pass. Out-of-work men took off their caps. Women cried. Then someone near the front started singing –

> Around the throne of God in heaven
> Thousands of children stand,
> Children whose sins are all forgiven,
> A holy, happy band …

Slowly, others started to join in and soon we were all singing that sad, triumphant hymn as we made our way down Market Street, into Eastgate and on to Cemetery Road. I felt lifted on a wave of emotion that thrilled me. It was a sensation not experienced before. At this pitch I wanted the funeral to go on for ever. Why couldn't days like this happen more often? This was even better than having the chicken-house on fire. This drama had more ceremony, more spectators.

It was only when we threw our flowers into the grave and the preacher dropped some gravel on to the lid of the coffin that I realized that we would never see this girl again, never share with her the model Garden of Gethsemane, or hold hands during prayers. She had gone, was lost, drowned under our wilting flowers and the mound of earth. Somehow, out of that darkness, out of that hole in Whittlesey, she was 'going to be with Jesus' and have everlasting life. Is that what was meant by miracles? I was puzzled by it all and for weeks after, whenever we passed that child's house, I stared in through the window to see if she was still there, propped up in bed with all our flowers round her.

After the funeral we walked back to our homes, knowing the drama was over. The bells of St Mary's were chiming one of the secular tunes that were played each day at nine, twelve, three and six. Tomorrow would be back to normal. What I could not fully appreciate was that such a day had not really been out of the ordinary. There were funerals on most days and the town would just continue with its births, deaths, marriages, work, school, parades, festivals, brickyards and harvest, and all the other things that went on making its own history as regularly as clockwork. The shops would still be there, the ice-cream man with his donkey and cart, the blacksmith in his forge, the recreation ground with its swings and roundabouts, the markets and fairs would still be there. Only the children would be different, taking our places as we grew up; finding out for themselves what it was like to belong to a town, unconcerned about anyone recording those daily events.

The hushed tones of mourning stayed with us for the rest of that day and in the evening we sat round our table quietly reading or talking. The table had a green velvet cloth with tassels and the room was lit only by an oil-lamp which stood in the centre. The softness of this light spread like a pool across the table until it reached the shadows at the edge. If moments can also be timeless, those moments encompassed us within the day's own eternity. They passed beyond our conscious awareness, just as we moved eventually away from the table. But the circle of faces framed in the silent light did not cease to exist. They were absorbed into the memory. The scene has become for me a painting by one of the great masters. All I have to do is pull back a curtain and there it is, as it always will be, glowing in its private stillness.

Although the world was a much quieter place fifty years ago than it is now it is a mistake to believe that it was as quiet as we like to remember. There were periods of the day, it is true, when one could be assured of a certain stillness, but long periods of silence were not that common. It was a different kind of noise – and more acceptable than most of the insults our ears have to tolerate today. When Mr Gale's threshing-tackle and steam-roller went down the street it made a considerable clatter. When a team of Suffolk Punches trotted by with their harness jangling and the iron-rimmed cartwheels clanking on the road, they disturbed any silence there might have been. It was a custom in those days, if someone in the street was seriously ill in bed, for the family to strew the road outside the house with straw so as to muffle the noise made by such vehicles. Tradesmen also made a habit of calling out their wares long before they reached the house. And the two churches not only volleyed off each hour with chimes but recognized the quarter-hours as well. But all these sounds were part of the daily pattern of our lives, not noise for the sake of noise.

It was a custom then for tradesmen to advertise their services in verse, displayed either above the shop or in the window. One, a chimney-sweep, had a notice on the front of his house which read –

AARON HALLAM, HE LIVES HERE,
SWEEPS ALL CHIMNEYS CLEAN AND CLEAR,
AND IN CASE THEY CATCH ON FIRE,
HE'LL PUT THEM OUT AT YOUR DESIRE!

(BLACK FLOUR SOLD HERE! WHITE FLOUR AT THE BAKERS)

It was also fashionable for people to have notices hanging in their houses, offering some crumb of wisdom. We had two in our front room which said, 'Home Is The Place Where You Grumble The Most But Are Treated the Best!' and 'As You Know A Bird By Its Note, So Do You Know A Man By His Conversation!' Rhymes and quotations were a much greater part of everyday life sixty years ago and even illiterate people could recite several ballads or monologues. 'The Touch of the Master's Hand' and 'A Madman's Will' were two we often heard at chapel anniversaries.

Although I was getting to know more about the town it was still our own street that provided me with most of my experiences. It was there where I saw the barrel-organ grinder churning out his hurdy-gurdy tunes for hours in the hope of getting a few coins dropped into his collecting-box. He was a small man with a black moustache and a bowler-hat who could easily have been mistaken for Charlie Chaplin. Sometimes he had a monkey with him who danced upon the organ as he played. Even the monkey looked underfed and sad, restricted as it was to a life upon a chain. One year the man and his barrel-organ came alone and when I asked him where his monkey was he said, without a flicker of expression, 'It died.'

Another figure who frequented Church Street then was the windmill man. He walked down the street singing 'Bring me your jamjars and any old clothes, and I'll give you windmills.' Then he would sit at the end of Thoroughfare Lane, through which the children went to school, and wait. The clothes could not have been worth much by the time he got them, but neither were his fragile windmills which usually came to pieces by the end of the day. They were only made of coloured paper, stuck on to a stick with a pin, but the sails went whirring round while we stood watching him and we always busied ourselves collecting jamjars or rags to exchange for one of these toys. A few days later, when he was miles away singing his song to someone else, our windmills broke or came undone, their sails like a withered flower. We used the sticks then for arrows or, in disgust, threw them on the fire. But we still went on collecting jamjars for the man who sat in Thoroughfare Lane until one year he, too, never returned with his coloured sails and empty promises.

There were other visitors, like the men who were survivors of the First World War, who came selling mops, bootlaces and pegs, and wore their medals as if to prove they had once been heroes. Some begged for water in their billy-cans, others asked for a meal. Tramps, vagrants, labourers out of work, Irishmen who came for the potato harvest, road-menders and gypsies, all cast a shadow on the street and we felt sorry that we could do no more for them. At least we had a roof over our heads, even if it leaked, and we had fire and bread.

One day, when it poured with rain for hours, a tramp

crouched by the wall of the house opposite and stayed there
until nearly dark. Each time we looked out he was there,
hunched in his long overcoat against the rain; a shadow who
would not go away. Mother wanted to ask him into the
house but was afraid. I stood by the window, watching first
the little armada of boats made by the heavy splashes of rain,
then the man who had nowhere to go. The rain ran off his hat
on to his shoulders but he was indifferent to it. I was about to
turn away when I saw a woman running across the road. She
had a towel over her head and a jug of tea in her hand. I had
not heard mother close the door. When she came back into
the house she did not say anything but hung the wet towel to
dry on the fireguard and went on preparing father's tea. As it
grew darker and the yellow gaslights came on in the street, I
looked out once more to see if the tramp was still there. But
the shadow had gone.

He was luckier than some. One morning we found a man
in our gateway who we thought had gone to sleep but, when
no one could wake him, one of our neighbours sent for the
doctor. Then the police came and later two men arrived with
blankets and a cart to take the stranger to the mortuary. By
the end of the day we were still talking about him and it was a
relief to pull down the window-blinds and shut out the street
– and the staring eyes of men with nowhere to go.

One of the games we played on winter nights was Creation
or Shadowgraph, in which the window-blind became the
screen on which we projected shadows made by our hands.
Crossing them palms upward so that the thumbs became a
bird's head, we saw great eagles rise from out of the
flowerpot, or pterodactyls flap from off the stairs. One hand
in profile, fingers parted like jaws, could make a horse or dog
or, closed and twisted from the wrist, produce a swan. A
clenched fist soon became Popeye-the-Sailorman or Mother
Riley. In gentler mood our fluttering hands were angels or
butterflies as we spent another evening pretending we were
God.

In the morning the familiarity of the street returned with its
usual sounds and callers – Dora, the milk-girl; Mr Popely, the
postman, Mr Crowson, the coalman; Mr Brown for the
insurance; Mr Ashby, the grocer; my grandfather, aunties; or
neighbouring children asking if I could go out to play.

I am not sure how old I was when my mother took me with her in the evening to witness the end-of-harvest ritual of gleaning. It was certainly before I started school and I can remember being wheeled down to the fields in my pram but, as this vehicle was also required for carrying home the filled sacks, it does not mean that I was still a baby. I would have been about four years old, I think.

The whole town took an interest in the harvest. It was the one time of the year when trades-people could expect to be paid, and it was also the time when the extra shopping was done for the winter months ahead. Harvest meant new boots, dresses, gardening-tools, or whatever could not be afforded at other times of the year. So when the steam-engines and threshing-tackle trundled down the street we knew it would not be long before we also went gleaning.

Our neighbours, like us, waited eagerly for the last stook (called 'the policeman') to be taken away from the gate to the field for this indicated that the farmer had now given permission for us to go on to his land.

Gleaning usually took place in the early evenings when the men and women were home from work. I looked forward to these excursions for I loved being out in the fens at such a time, when they had a deeper sense of mystery than they had at midday.

Once we were safely in the field I was allowed to run about and collect my own handful of wheat-ears to put in the sack. The smell of the earth, the sharp corn-stubble, the distant brickyard chimneys like pencil-marks on the sky, remain vivid moments of perception. Even at that age I knew that I was where I belonged and that each moment was part of a long history. I remember, too, on one occasion being awe-struck as a deep orange moon rose out of the misty horizon. It rose like a god from secret waters, still dripping wet; huge, full and breathing. It was like watching the birth of a new world, virgin and uninhabited; a giant traveller from outer space. What must our first fathers have thought, I wonder, when they saw such a spectacle arriving into their sky from nowhere? I know I saw it then, my eyes big with wonder, and have seen it hundreds of times since with the same primitive excitement. For a few moments it looked as if the moon was too heavy to lift itself from the abyss beyond the horizon. Then, slowly, out of the deepening mist, it heaved itself into the sky until it grew smaller and golden, far enough away now to be safe.

By the time I had taken my eyes off it the gleaners on earth had finished, the pram was stacked with its full sacks, and we were ready to go home.

After the harvest it was as if we stepped straight into winter.

4 Somewhere like Hunstan, Heacham or Snettisham

Having found the box of old photographs I am not always certain now which comes first – the memory or the reminder. I have written of those early years of my childhood before, so I do believe that my memory is accurate. What the photographs now do is to sharpen the recall of each experience, as if a veil is finally removed to reveal the full extent of the joy, or pain, of the memory. Where the photographs are most useful is in the dates which someone sensibly pencilled on the back. Fixing the year in this way helps me to stand back and see myself from a distance, as in a snapshot taken at Heacham in 1933 –

There is a boy, no more than three, standing in the shallow waters of a muddy sea, believing it to be the biggest sea in the world, beyond which there is no other land. He can feel the gentle waves tugging at his feet and knows that if his father did not hold him tightly by the hand he would float away on the next tide, never to be seen again. The father is ageless – as fathers always are – and wears a brown waistcoat even in the sea. His trousers are rolled up to the knees and he smiles happily at the camera, knowing that two or three steps will bring him back to land. At his other side is a girl, no more than eight, who is also smiling. But the boy has that distrustful, frowning stare that no reassurance can dispel.

Is that really me? It must be, for I recognize my father and my sister, but the small boy is a stranger who has somehow wandered into one of our holiday snaps taken in Norfolk nearly sixty years ago. There we are, a normal family on holiday before the world was changed, standing in the shallow ripples of a tideless sea, smiling forever into a

Brownie camera that is a museum-piece itself now. There is another picture which includes my mother, with her dress tucked into her knee-length drawers. Father's knees look as if they are held up by braces. My sister and I have baggy swimsuits which sag at the crotch, as if we had both just had an accident. I can smell the seaweed, cockles and wet clothes of all our holidays, whether they were at Heacham, Hunstanton, Skegness or Cromer. For a moment I am surrounded by fishing-nets, sand-castles, buckets and spades, and the picnic-basket is full of sandwiches, packets of crisps (each with its own little bag of salt), and there are bars of Fry's peppermint-cream chocolate and jars of ginger-beer. There are the sounds too. Distant voices are thrown about in the wind. The waves begin to nibble at the shore. A little red aeroplane flies over, trailing an advertisement for Sunlight Soap, and a man plays a banjo. There was sound but not noise, at least not as we know it now. The world *was* a quieter place then and there was more space – both in the sky and on the beach. Has someone breathed on the photographs and brought them back to life? It feels so.

Not all the photographs are of holidays. There is one of my father when he was nineteen which shows him as a slim, dapper young man with thick black hair, starched collar and drainpipe trousers. As I ever only knew him as a stout man who needed large, loose-fitting trousers, I find this picture a difficult one to accept; not, maybe, as difficult as the one of me at the age of twelve months in a frilly white dress, sitting in a white wicker-chair, chubby-faced and with a mop of black curls, and already staring mutinously at the camera. Was the dress simply a hand-me-down from my sister or, having lost her first son, was mother hoping for another girl? I was told later that she had always wanted a son, so why the dress, ribbons and curly hair?

As with my mother, during the last weeks of her final illness, so too had I sat with my father when he was in hospital, talking about our life together. It was not the recent happenings that occupied his thoughts but the events of years far off. In his latter years father could not remember anything that happened two days ago but his memory was clear about his own childhood, and mine. Sitting by his bed in that dimly lit ward late at night was to take a journey back into the past.

The future no longer mattered. The present was a waiting time, like waiting for the expected turn of the tide, or a fire to go out. Although he craved to go home I am sure that in his lucid moments my father knew that his life was nearly over. When his mind wandered he relived episodes from days I had forgotten all about –

My father, who'd not smoked for forty years,
    sat on his death-bed puffing mock cigars
and blowing smoke-rings down the midnight ward
    like tiny haloes flying without wings.

He did not speak but smiled and gently waved
    at someone opposite who was not there.
The pain had left him as his mind returned
    to days when he was young, with strength to spare.

Within his tight-skinned skull already cold
    he felt the sun and heard the laughing sea
where he'd gone paddling on his one week off,
    his work-day trousers rolled up to the knee.

I tried to talk but something in my throat
    choked back the words for I was now a child
clutching his hand as I did then, afraid
    of what might happen should I lose my hold.

I watched his fingers stiffen round my own,
    his staring eyes withdraw, the smoke-rings fade.
And, in the low-lit ward beyond his death,
    felt the first shudder of the turning tide.

I had not anticipated the impact of such a moment when one is suddenly aware of being the head of the next generation.

The snapshot of our Heacham holiday only served to reawaken many other memories, like the one of the summer of 1936, when we could not afford to stay at a boarding-house but went instead for 'days only' to different places, taking our own food with us. I quite enjoyed this kind of holiday because it meant we had several train journeys in one week rather than just the one. Indeed, the holiday started for me at Whittlesea Station. Although the spelling of the town was Whittle*sey*, the spelling used by the railway company was always Whittle*sea*. Both were correct, as the suffix *ey* or *ea* meant that our town had once been an island. And, as we were also in the Isle of Ely, it seemed appropriate that the station chose to identify itself with the coast. To pass the ticket office and to stand on the platform, with its gas-lamps, iron seats and row of red fire-buckets outside the Gents, was to feel the first thrill of adventure. Then the porter looked at his watch, glanced up at the signals and said 'She's on her way.' Soon the first puff of smoke appeared over the trees and we heard the sound of the wheels on the rails, and finally the train came into view and slithered expertly to a standstill. We climbed in, settled ourselves down on the high-backed seats and waited for the whistle to blow. A snort of steam, a tugging of carriages, and we were off.

The carriages had no corridors. Passengers sat four each side of the compartment on hard button-cloth seats and stared at each other. My first interest was to look at the water-colour paintings which hung above the seats. They were usually of castles or harbours and the memory of them now evokes the mood of those days almost as much as the holidays themselves. Above the pictures were the cord luggage-racks, sagging from years of use. On to these would go our buckets, spades, beach-ball, picnic-basket and raincoats.

When I had finished looking at the pictures I turned my attention to the window, puzzled again by the rise and fall of the telegraph-wires as we sped along. It gave me a sense of flying, as if the train was hedge-hopping over the fens. 'If you can't count twelve between each pole', said Mr Coles the gate-keeper, 'you're travelling at more than sixty miles an hour.' He didn't say how fast you had to count but I was convinced that no one else had travelled faster.

As smoke from the engine flapped past the window I began to dream of the sea and the great stretch of beach. Beyond the trampolining telegraph-wires the fenland fields went on ripening under the July sun, mile after mile of space and sky as we raced through Cambridgeshire and Norfolk until we reached Hunstanton. There again were the waves, the pier, the smell of seaweed and cockles, the lure of slot-machines and the weary donkeys waiting to receive the next Roy Rogers. It was as if we had come home rather than left home.

Hunstanton, Heacham, Snettisham, Cromer or Great Yarmouth, each in their turn provided us with a week's holiday for which my parents had saved all year. Apart from the rare occasion we managed to book in at a boarding-house which had been recommended to us or had advertised itself in the local papers. Once we rented a beach bungalow and catered for ourselves but I remember better some of the boarding-houses. Wherever they were they were much the same — 'Sea View', 'Cliff View', 'Ocean Prospect', 'Sandyways', or 'Sunningfield', all displaying window-cards saying 'VACANCIES' and 'CHILDREN WELCOME'.

Walking into the house of our choice I gazed nervously at its size and began to worry about the other guests. The hall was covered with heavy wallpaper patterned with roses. The barometer had a notice underneath which said 'DO NOT TAP', the antler-hatstand held walking-sticks, umbrellas and a butterfly-net, and steep stairs led to a landing with several doors. Which one was ours? Whose were the others?

Then into the bedroom with its towering wardrobe and marbled wash-stand, and that peculiar boarding-house smell that always evoked a mixture of all the smells of all the human beings who had ever stayed there. Pinned to the inside of the bedroom door was a handwritten notice telling us what time we had to be in by each night, what times the meals were served, and at what time we had to vacate the room the following Saturday.

From the window I looked out expecting the sea to be lapping at the garden gate. It was usually far off in the distance, glimpsed between roof-tops and at least ten minutes walk after breakfast. All I could see close at hand was the rest of the street, its pavements dusty with sand, the walls scurvy with salt. The dining-rooms always seemed to contain one fat lady with earrings, two lean ladies in black who seldom spoke, and a man with a ginger moustache and a boil on his neck, who always winked at me after pulling a face at one of the ladies.

There is one photograph which I cannot identify. It had no date and was obviously taken by a promenade photographer. It must have been 1937 but I do not know whether it was at

Great Yarmouth or Skegness. We are all walking along the promenade – father in a three-piece suit and carrying a newspaper; mother pushing my two-year-old brother in a push-chair; my sister already looking grown-up with a handbag under her arm, and me – cocky and toothless as I smiled at the photographer who caught that brief moment in our lives. Behind us are strangers, young men of eighteen or nineteen who, a few years later, were doubtless called up to fight in a war we still did not believe could happen.

Is that what those summers were – all part of a dream, where the sun always shone and the sky was permanently blue? The summers of the thirties were exceptionally good ones, with low rainfalls, long heatwaves and droughts. Our holidays, in the most gentle way, branded themselves on to our memories. I did not know then that there were three million people out of work, nor that this was to be one of the last holidays I was to spend with my family.

One day, as he lay in hospital waiting for an X-ray, my father said to me, 'I could just eat a nice Yarmouth bloater now, or some cockles from Hunstanton. Could you get me some?' It was almost his last contact with the past and there were tears in his eyes when he said, 'we had some good summers.' He died in hospital at the age of eighty-five, a few months before my mother. After sixty-three years together neither could bear to survive without the other for long. They were possessively devoted to each other and never craved for more than what their simple life had to offer.

Only now, with all the changes there have been in recent years, can I fully appreciate that it was a very different world before 1939. The old photographs have reminded me of several incidents that I can now place in some sort of chronological order but there are still some memories for which there are no photographs, nor can I place them with any accuracy in my years as a child. Was I, as a baby, held by our neighbours under the cold water-tap outside our back door, or is that some fragment of a nightmare I once had? The thought returns to me frequently and I can clearly see myself, naked as a suckling pig on a spit, being held by two women and turned over and over under the cold running water while they laughed. But why? It was not meant to be cruel, I'm sure of that. And where was my mother, for I am equally certain she was not one of the women. Yet I hear myself crying and feel again the fear of water drowning me. And did I ever get shut in a high, windowless room from which there was no exit? I knew of no such place but still have dreams of climbing up steep spiral stone stairs until I squeezed through a narrow aperture into that small cell from which there was no escape. And did I really try to bury myself in the garden one morning because I was afraid to own up that I had broken a vase full of flowers? Such images recur frequently, as if the child I still cannot get to know is haunting me, trailing at my heels, hiding round the next corner. I was disturbed by things I could not understand and even at that age was vaguely aware of being caught in a web of superstitions, beliefs, prejudices, doubts and attitudes whose strands were to vibrate in my memory for many years. The house itself was full of moods, its cupboards full of the past, with creaks, groans and ticking sounds that came from, what? Not ticking-spiders, I hoped, for I had been told that ticking-spiders were a sure warning of a death in the house. A crow sitting on the chimney-pot was another, or a falling star, or a dead frog on the doorstep. Such fears did not only concern death itself but also the life hereafter. When my grandmother died some years later, I was expected to kiss her cold face as she lay in her coffin so that I should not be haunted by her ghost. Nor should I turn my back on the solitary candle-flame that burned day and night in the room where the corpse lay before burial. To do so would take a day out of my own life for every step I took from the room. These were also times when all the clocks in the house were stopped and pennies placed on the dead person's eyes, cotton-wool stuffed up his or her nostrils, and the family went into mourning for a month. Compared with all these threats the bad luck that would come by treading on a spider or even the cracks in a paved path, or the putting of shoes on the table, was bearable. Crossed knives, walking under ladders, two spoons in a saucer, or cutting one's nails on Sunday, added variety to the calamities that awaited us if we put a foot wrong.

Living in a crowded house, where only the outer doors were ever closed, I heard all kinds of conversations and opinions expressed. My father's ideas were fixed, both in

politics and religion. As a lifelong nonconformist he had no
time for the Church of England. As a lifelong Socialist he had
no time for the Tories, all of whom were tarred with the same
blue brush and contemptuously dismissed as 'toadies'. Only
people who worked with their hands knew what hard work
was and if you didn't look after yourself, no one would do it
for you. But he was a generous man with a lovely, earthy
sense of humour. He enjoyed hearing funny stories and
delighted even more in telling them. As a young man he had
enjoyed playing football, was fond of ballroom dancing and
ice-skating but, during my childhood, his great passion was
brass-banding.

Several of the photographs in the shoe-box were of the
King's Dyke Silver Prize Band, with whom he played second
trombone. There were photographs of the whole band, with
their guest-conductor who prepared them for contests;
photographs of the band at the Crystal Palace after they had
won first prize in the fourth section; photographs of just the
three trombones, with my father proud in his uniform, the
nine brass buttons on his tunic shining, like his boots,
forever.

Brass-band music was as natural to my world as was
chapel, medicine, Yorkshire-pudding on Sundays, and carols
at Christmas. Just as I inherited that love from my father, so he
had inherited it from his. Grandad had a passion for music,
which he could read far better than the written word, and he
possessed several cylinder recordings of light and classical
music. He believed that he was one of the first people in
Whittlesey to own a gramophone and the distorted voice at
the beginning of each cylinder: 'This is an Edison Bell
Recording', crackled out of the convolvulous horn from
which the music followed. He later graduated to a wind-up
machine with shellac discs and steel needles and the sound
was so improved he thought he was sitting in the Queen's
Hall listening to the real thing. What he would say about
today's compact discs is not hard to imagine. They would be
a miracle beyond his comprehension, just as television or the
telephone would be to anyone of his generation. He was a
good player of most brass instruments, from the cornet to the
sousaphone, and had been the bandmaster of bands in
London as well as Whittlesey. My father often told us that his

father played the cornet so sweetly that he could lull his children to sleep when everything else failed.

I was soon given my first instrument, a rather battered second-hand trombone but my arm was too short to reach all the shifts and I was transferred to the cornet. The names of famous championship bands such as St Hilda's, Besses-o'-the-Barn and Black Dyke Mills, were as familiar to me as first-division football teams. Where other boys found their heroes in Hobbs, Sutcliffe, Bradman, Stanley Matthews or Tommy Farr, I revered the names of men like Jack Mackintosh, Bert Sullivan and Harry Mortimer. Cornets, trombones, music-stands and metronomes, were an accepted part of the household furniture and hardly a day went by without there being some kind of music in our lives. In addition to the brass instruments we had the piano, and my sister was also learning to play the violin.

My father insisted that I had an hour's practice each day and this was frequently extended to two hours when, in the evenings, he decided to go through my exercises with me. The moment he saw that I was restless, or not doing anything, he would say, 'Right! Get your instrument out and let me see what you can do.'

I did not relish these moments because my playing rarely came up to his high expectations. His great ambition was to get me up to a standard where I could play with one of the top bands in the country. It was a wild dream. Slowly, and sighing heavily, I would take my music-stand from behind the piano, my cornet from its case, and fumble with the music until it rested safely in front of me. Then I would take another second or two to moisten my lips and get the embouchure right on the mouthpiece before playing the first note. Father was aware of these delaying tactics and would say, 'Come on, we haven't got all night.'

He always sat on a chair beside me, with a wooden stool on his knee, on which he beat time with a steel ruler, making sure that I kept rigidly to the beat. If I failed, or played the wrong note, the ruler would leap unerringly from the stool to my thigh and he would snap, 'Listen to the beat! What d'you think I'm here for!' Or he would correct my fingering, saying, 'Can't you tell the difference between A-flat or A-sharp? A-flat is second and third valve. Start again.' And back to the beginning I had to go, time and time again, until I got the piece right. On one occasion he said, 'It's about time you pulled your socks up, otherwise you'll get nowhere.' Not knowing what he meant I put my cornet down on the table and bent over to pull up my socks. It was more than he could bear. He threw his beating-stick on to the table and burst out laughing. 'You're not only unmusical, you're simple as well.' It was only a slight reprieve. Seriousness soon came back into my lesson and the threatening beat of the ruler continued on the stool for another half-hour. Once we went on so late at night that the neighbours complained, so for the next few evenings, I used a mute in the bell of my instrument to reduce the noise. My father may have been an enthusiastic teacher but he was not a very patient one. Nor could he always illustrate what he wanted. He was always telling me about the importance of getting a good tone but never able to tell me how this could be achieved. 'You sound more like a sick bull', he said one day but, fortunately for me, grandfather had just arrived and said, 'I'd give him a rest from those exercises if I were you, Ted. He wants melodies now. That's what'll improve his tone. Try him on Handel's *Largo*, or 'Silver threads among the gold' ... Then he turned to me. 'Any fool can play notes, boy. You have to be good to make music. Don't just blow. Make your instrument sing. Think of the words. A good player could make that cornet speak.'

From then on I played mostly music that had words and had to learn them as well as the notes. But my practices were at least more interesting and several of my school-mates used to gather outside our window to hear me play. They could not understand why I preferred playing my cornet to kicking a football, but they no longer made fun of me, especially when I told them that one day I was going to play a solo in London. I was never long on modesty and the hours I spent in my own company allowed me to have the most extravagant daydreams.

My father's band occasionally gave Sunday evening concerts in the gardens of a local solicitor, who let his grounds be used free of charge so that all the money raised could go to a charity. One of the most popular events of the year was 'Hospital Sunday', the proceeds from which supported the hospitals at Doddington and Peterborough.

The phrase 'Hospital Sunday' worried me for some time when I was a child because the word *hospital* was always pronounced as *horse-piddle* and, although we regularly had horses relieving themselves in the street, I could not understand why we needed a special Sunday to commemorate their deeds.

While the band played, I wandered about among the flower-beds and trees, mesmerized by the smells from the borders of nicotiana or lavender, overawed by the size of the cedar trees, and a little scared of the shadows in the shrubbery. The further away I moved from the band the more haunting became the sound. Few people actually listened to the music. It was a time to talk about old harvests, feasts, floods, fishing, poaching, and those characters who were already legends in the town. But we always knew when the concert was about to end for the band's last item never changed from one year to the next. They always played 'Deep Harmony' and, as that memorable sound melted into the tired and lazy night, the crowd started drifting away, dropping a few coins into the pudding-bowl provided at the gate for the collection.

But already the photographs have disrupted the chronology of events and I must attempt some further ordering from memory. What else happened between 1930 and the fading tunes which were played in those tranquil gardens before the commencement of the Second World War?

1935–40

5 A memory of pomegranates

A walk round the town brings back as many memories as does the box of photographs and although much has changed there are still many visible reminders of that pre-war world. The primary school I attended is now a snooker hall, the senior school in Station Road is now the Roman Catholic church. I miss some of the old-fashioned shops like Delahoy and Walker and Manns, and several of the pubs have disappeared. But the sixteenth-century stone buttercross is still there and that in itself can bring back events which the town will not see again. Sunday School outings usually started from the market-place. Each denomination would gather its young round the buttercross ready for the grand march down to the station. We wore small bows of different coloured ribbons to indicate which Sunday School we belonged to and clutched our buckets and spades for fear of having them snatched from us by some less fortunate child. There was always confusion, always a few tears as tempers frayed or someone remembered they had left something at home, and it seemed ages before we reached the train waiting to take us to Hunstanton. The calamities did not end there. One year my mother was unable to accompany us and I was put in the care of my grandmother. We had been on the beach no more than five minutes when I fell into the sea, fully-clothed, and had to be hauled out, wailing loudly from my close proximity with eternity. Grandmother was not amused. She stripped me of my clothes and spread them to dry over the surrounding rocks. The rest of the children in my class stood gawping at me, tittering hideously at my embarrassment until grandma smothered me in a large towel and told the spectators to 'clear off'. I do not think that the rest of the day could have been much of a success because I

can remember nothing more. It was the one year when I felt
my hundred per cent attendance at Sunday School had not
been fairly rewarded. Fortunately no one was on hand with a
camera to record that humiliation for the shoe-box.

There is a photograph of our chapel's harvest festival in
1920 which reminds me of the many I was to know later. All
the produce is displayed on trestle-tables between the
choir-seats, just under the pulpit. From the look of all the
vegetables, fruit, sheaves of corn and other gifts, it must have
been a good summer.

Like the Sunday School outings, harvest festivals were
anticipated and prepared for with tremendous enthusiasm.
Vegetables were coaxed to perfection and flowers protected
by paper bags or butterfly-nets so that none of the petals
would be bruised. Only the best of what had been grown was
good enough to give to the chapel. Harvest festivals, like
other religious events in the town, were highly competitive.
Marrows and pumpkins were especially popular because, as
well as their size, they had the added novelty of being
engraved with a text from the bible, or a line from a hymn.
These were scratched on in the early stages of growth so that
by the time the vegetable was fully grown the letters stood
out clear and bold on the hard skin, as if Moses himself had
chiselled them there. Had he done so perhaps the spelling
might have been a little better and the words would have
appeared more often in the right order. On one occasion a
phrase from William Cowper's hymn 'How Sweet the Name
of Jesus Sounds', which should have read ''Tis manna to the
troubled breast / And to the weary rest ...' came out as ''Tis
manner to the troubled breast / And weary to the rest ...'
There was also a marrow which extolled us to 'Love thy
enemy as they Fiend' and one which was meant to encourage
us in constant prayer but only succeeded in telling us to 'Pay
without ceasing.'

Such errors were soon forgiven by the congregation who,
having had a good laugh, went on to admire the rest of the
offerings – parsnips, beetroot, carrots, celery, jellies,
sponge-cakes, jars of home-made chutney and jam, bunches
of grapes, baskets of oranges, packets of figs, sprays of
dahlias and chrysanthemums, and exotic things like pomegra-
nates. One attraction was always a huge harvest loaf shaped

like a sheaf of corn, which was baked and donated by one of the town's bakers. Sacks of potatoes were also given by local farmers and the coalman in our street always gave one hundredweight of coal.

For the children, the greatest fun of harvest festivals came with the sale of the produce on the Monday evening. Everything was carried into the schoolroom and then auctioned off by a member of the chapel choir who was very skilled at making you pay twice as much as you would have been charged for the same item in the shops. But, as it was all in aid of the chapel funds, no one minded. I was satisfied if I came away with my annual pomegranate which spoke to me of Solomon's Temple or the Gardens of Babylon. When, fifty years later, I picked one off a tree in Greece it was as if I had just arrived at the end of a long journey.

Another photograph, dated Sunday, August 1936 reminds me of other events on the market-place, this time an open air service where a crowd of people have gathered to hear a visiting preacher. He is using for his pulpit something that looks like a farm-cart and I can remember being taken to hear him on more than one occasion. He was a striking-looking man with white hair and a bushy moustache, not unlike Lloyd George in appearance and with the same gift of oratory. Whether he preached doctrinally good sermons I cannot say but I do know he made me feel hot and cold by his stirring use of language. His timing was perfect. In the middle of a dramatic phrase he would pause, with his hand raised, and in the silence we could hear St Mary's clock ticking reprovingly until the rest of the preacher's sentence shattered the tension with its threat of doom. The crowds were also the same. Men in rough cloth suits for Sunday, their thumbs stuffed into thick leather belts. Women, grouped together, arms folded or holding an infant, shrinking at the wrath of God that was to come. Drink, tobacco, gambling, adultery, lying and cheating, worldly pleasures and vices of the flesh were, we were told, all stepping-stones to the fiery pit of hell. Wealth, greed, incest and fornication were the gateways to eternal damnation. By the time his list was finished we knew that very few, if any, of the town's population would ever make it to heaven. Then, after a final hymn, the crowd dispersed, either to the pubs or the cramped houses from which it had come, assured in the knowledge that the 'Carthorse Preacher' would be back in a few weeks' time to plead for their conversion again. It was all rousing stuff and, had there been a little more of that 'fire and brimstone' preaching in later years not so many of the local places of worship would have been forced to close down or survive only for the faithful few.

Not all our Sunday entertainment was religious. We moved from the sacred to the secular with remarkable agility. As well as the 'Hospital Sundays' and the band concerts in Mr Bowker's gardens, there were street parades when men with blackened faces and funny costumes jangled money-boxes from door to door, clowning their way down the street and making everybody laugh. Some of the men had large false busts made of balloons, or bras made from saucepan-lids. They blew whistles and bazookas, whirled rattles and scraped at wash-boards, and kissed every woman in sight. After them came the town band which led the official procession, followed by the St John's Ambulance Brigade, the Red Cross, the Police Force, the Fire Brigade, the Oddfellows, Boy Scouts, Girl Guides, and anyone else who wanted to join in this noisy parade making its way to the Manor Field for a brief outdoor service at which we inevitably sang 'O God, Our Help in Ages Past', and 'Abide with Me'.

There were the national celebrations too which gave our town the opportunity to prove that fenmen are not incapable of enjoying themselves. Our street, like every other street in Britain, had a wonderful time celebrating the coronation of King George VI and Queen Elizabeth in 1937. I still have the souvenir mug I was given at our street party. The abdication of Edward VIII the previous year had caused more than a stir in our community which was not wholly royalist. It was the topic of conversation on the doorsteps, at shop counters, in barbers' chairs and public bars for weeks. I remember we sat round our wireless-set to hear the king explain to the nation why he had decided to give up his throne. My father was scathing in his criticism of a man who could sacrifice his historic inheritance for a married woman – and an American at that! I think he came close to changing my own first name, which was a surprising choice anyway, as he was never a royalist.

Like most children, I enjoyed a good street party when the houses were festooned with bunting and Union Jacks hung from bedroom windows. What could a seven-year-old know about the Means Test, or that Hitler was already changing the world for everyone in his own ruthless, clinical way? What did I know of soup-kitchens, the Jarrow March, the empty shipyards, or that children were being bombed in Spain? My world ended where the horizon separated the earth from sky. I could not see the smoke rising from the piles of books being burnt in Germany. I could not hear the rantings of Mussolini, or Mosley.

Not only were we, as yet, untouched by these changes in history, but I now had a new source of freedom – a bike. The bike did not so much arrive, it grew. For weeks the bits and pieces had been slowly accumulating in the wash-house – the frame, wheels, pedals, mudguards, brakes and a bell. When father thought I was not around he worked at putting it all together in the hope that it would appear as a surprise. The finished machine both pleased and frightened me and for the next few evenings I was taken out to Ramsey Road to learn how to ride it. To begin with my father kept me upright by holding on to the back of the seat. I was nervous and kept asking for a reassurance that he was still there. The moment I started to wobble I would shout, 'Are you still holding on?' Then I would start to feel the bike suddenly right itself. For a week I collected enough cuts, bruises and bumps to last for the rest of childhood. One evening, when the controlling hand of father was not where it should have been, I overshot the grass verge and disappeared head-first into a dyke full of stinging nettles and barbed-wire. The more I struggled to get out, the more I became entangled in the wire, and the more my flesh absorbed the burning stings from the nettles. This was surely a foretaste of hell. My face blazed with its fires, my hands burst out of their skins, even the handlebars of the bike itself became the horns of Satan. When I was pulled out by my father, all he said was, 'What made you go and do a thing like that for? I spent weeks getting that bike ready for you. Now look at it!'

'Sorry!'

'What on earth your mother's going to say when we get home I daresn't think.'

'It's all your fault', I said. 'You shouldn't have let go.'

'I can't hold on to you forever.' He looked down at the bike. 'Come on, pick it up.'

Then, having straightened the handlebars, untwisted the mudguards and adjusted the seat, he made me get on again to ride home. 'You can't give in just because of one little fall, so stop snivelling.'

All went well until we reached our street, by which time father had decided that I was now making such good progress that I could be left on my own again. I only became aware of his hand not holding me when I realized that his voice was becoming more and more distant. But my fear was quickly dismissed by the sudden sense of triumph I now had that I could actually ride a bike. I pedalled faster, determined to arrive home in style. The gateway leading to the backs of our houses was at least eight feet wide, wide enough to get two farm-carts through at a push. But, as I turned from the road, this space rapidly shrank and I panicked. I missed the gateway by three feet and went into the wall of our neighbour's house, hurling myself once more over the handlebars and into the bricks.

Father rushed towards me. 'You stupid little ...' He was either lost for words or did not want to use the one that came to mind. 'I never thought I'd have such an idiot as a son', he said with a doom-laden sigh.

We went into the yard, propped up the bike against the iron rain-water tub and crept into the house. Mother took one look at me and turned to father. 'Good Lord! What have you been trying to do? Kill him?'

'It's nothing. You have to expect a scratch or two when you're learning to ride a bike.'

'Scratch or two! He looks as if he's been on the Somme battlefront. I told you all along he'd be no blessed good on the thing.' Then she turned to me. 'Come here and let's have a look at you ... That's the last time you go out on that thing even if I have to smash it to pieces myself. If you can't steer it through our gateway the next thing you'll be doing is putting yourself under a lorry ... Take your shirt off.'

She prepared a bowl of hot water clouded with Dettol and began bathing my wounds. The cleaning of my face was even more painful than the initial inflictions of the nettles and I began to squeal. Father returned the bike to the wash-house and did not appear back in the house until I'd been put to bed. I discovered later that he had been busy repairing my bike ready for the next lesson. I sat at the bedroom window, looking out at the garden, feeling a miserable failure. Again, in trying to please, I had tried too hard and was ashamed of myself.

Mother's threats to destroy the bike were soon forgotten and it was not long before I was able to ride out on my own whenever I wished. Now I was more free than ever before and, as I always preferred being alone, I went out as often as I could. Soon I could ride with only one hand on the handlebars, then no hands at all. I hung on to the tail-boards of passing farm vehicles to save pedalling, or placed myself in the slipstream of a lorry to gather more speed. Riding my bike became as natural as walking and it enabled me to go much further than Ramsey or Black Bush. Now I could get as far as Pondersbridge, Glassmoor Bank, Chapel Bridge or Cock Bank. The fields and sky were mine. I could sit on the banks of a river or dyke and wait for the appearance of a heron, kingfisher or otter, or I would watch the men and women working on the land, small and insignificant in so large a space, but all part of that slow, cumbersome masque that had been going on for centuries. This was where men once walked on stilts before the land was drained. This was where the fierce, stubborn character of the fenman was born. Today, the land cranes its neck to stare beyond the water-line and we walk on imaginary stilts to give our spirits height. A man who has looked upon this land knows his own mind. When heavy rain-clouds crouch on the horizon he is aware that the battle with nature is far from over. Bending over the clogged hilt of his spade, his braces straining across his back with all the tautness of a catapult, he feels his roots clutching the soil even when he looks up briefly at the sky. He is part of the earth. He is both present and past, birth and death, the blood and spittle of ten thousand years – and yet he knows his own breath is short. He says what he wants and he gets on with his work, for without him the fields would degenerate again into a wilderness or boggy place fit only for wild-fowl and fish. I watched them when I was a boy – beet-hoers, dyke-cleaners, men with scythes, women with hoes,

ploughmen and sowers, sensing their place in the fens' harsh
weft but unable to explain its purpose. They were like threads
in some ancient tapestry, or awkward movements in the
wind's dance. Without them the landscape would not be
complete. Later, when I found out that my task was to write,
I wanted to write about them and their habitation –

> I watched them ploughing the frost in
> to leaven the land, bright knuckles
> of steel kneading the black soil –
> a continuance of those tasks which
> broke earth's crust and still
> demand all that a man's worth.
>
> I thought I had come to see
> this transformation of the year as
> dandruff on the tired shoulders
> of summer. Yet, today, the fields
> are laid-out, groomed and brushed
> not for a funeral, but for a birth.
>
> Grey beards of reed twitch in the sun
> with the unshaken faith of Simeon.
> For them, no more than sleep separates
> winter from spring. But what will
> rise out of the dark, or burst
> from this buried frost then?
>
> Such questions they need never ask.
> They plough on while the light lasts,
> leaving philosophy to those
> who cannot accept that some seeds
> die, some germinate; that what survives
> is all that next year grows.

Riding back into the town was also a returning to the security
of a settlement which had not changed for centuries. Old Mr
Popple, the bespoke tailor in Whitmore Street, still sat
cross-legged in the window of his front room, like an ageing
Buddha stitching away as he had done for years, so that his
legs were permanently bowed when he stood up to walk. Mr
Theo Bingham's offal shop still exuded that lovely dry dusty
smell from its wooden bins and I always bought the bran

there for my rabbits. Miss Mann's shoe-shop with its smell of leather and Mr Mann's draper's shop that smelt of new underwear and gloves. Then there was the smell of newly made bread from the bakehouse on the corner of Church Street, and the smell of fish-and-chips. And there were the greengrocers, the butchers, the cobbler and the rag-and-bone man's yard, all adding their smells to a world which I believed could never change.

I should have known better because I had seen changes in the town, particularly when fire destroyed houses that had been there for hundreds of years. Whittlesey has a history of fire and has been devastated by it on numerous occasions. In April 1244 every house was burnt to the ground and the forty inhabitants perished. The village was rebuilt but, thirty years later, was again reduced to ashes when the narrow streets of thatched cottages went up in flames. Such tragedies continued well into the nineteenth century and a local newspaper report of 1809 says that, 'the dreadful fire consumed many houses and left scores of people homeless.' On 18 June 1870, the same paper reported, 'an alarming and destructive fire occured at Whittlesey. Eleven cottages were burned to the ground and an entire range of premises 150 yards long were reduced to a burning mass.' I can remember being taken to see two or three serious fires where rows of houses were burnt down and families stacked what was left of their furniture in the street. The smell can never be forgotten, nor the dejected, defeated and weeping faces of the victims. Mothers and children huddled together on the pavements while the uncontrollable fires consumed all they had possessed. One such fire was in our own street when a row of cottages just beyond St Andrew's Church was burnt down and the families had to find lodgings with relations or friends until they could be rehoused. The smoke of those fires stayed in our clothes for days and made the air rancid. Admittedly, the fire-fighting equipment in the town then was not very sophisticated and, in an area that had once been under water, water was often hard to find. I think before the Second World War the Whittlesey fire brigade still relied on horses to pull the tender and hand-pumps to fill the hose. Certainly when I had to play a popular piano piece called 'Fire! Fire!' I had plenty of experience to draw on for my interpretation.

6 Red cabbages, pickled walnuts and things

Something else which belongs to that decade before the Second World War is the innocence of childhood Christmasses when I believed in Santa Claus and miracles and looked forward to new toys and the kind of food that we never saw at any other time of the year.

I always knew when Christmas was getting near because a tone of secrecy crept into my parents' conversation and certain corners of the house were out-of-bounds, Smiles, confidences, warnings and requests all meant that for the next few weeks I had to live very warily. Any refusal to eat my meals or be quiet would be answered by the threat, 'Very well, you won't get anything for Christmas!'

Once, in an unwise tantrum, I said this didn't worry me at all as I didn't want anything for Christmas anyway. I was already out of favour for having thrown my favourite racing-car into the fire in a fit of temper and also subjecting my sister's doll to the same fate. I was given a good hiding and told that I did not deserve any presents and, unless I changed my ways, there wouldn't be any on Christmas morning. I was ever short-tempered and quick to explode, so I shouted up the chimney to an imaginary Santa Claus, saying, 'I hope you burn your arse!' The response from my mother was a few hefty smacks on my legs and an immediate sending to bed.

When that Christmas morning arrived and I found my pillow-case still empty at the foot of my bed, I realized the folly of my defiance. I could see that my sister's pillow-case was bulging with gifts and I could not keep my tears back for long. Howling with remorse I went into my parents' room and said, 'I'm sorry! I'm sorry!' Allowing a few moments in which to judge whether my feelings were sincere, my mother then opened the wardrobe door and pulled out a pillow-case as full as my sister's. I paused briefly to ponder on how it came to be there and then went back to my own room to see what had been left for me.

I always enjoyed Christmas, especially Christmas Eve. Having gone to bed I would lie awake listening to the sounds that came from the waiting town – people going home from the pubs: St Mary's bells trying to out-ring those of St Andrew's; the chapel choir and, later, the sound of the town band as it played carols – first at the big houses, then at the chosen section of each street. My father was band treasurer at the time and was canny enough to plan the order of calls so that the first donations entered into his book had to be matched by the rest of the gentry they visited. When it came to the ordinary street collections he was not as calculating. For quite a few years they did not collect on Christmas Eve at all but went round in the New Year to receive donations. My father loved carolling and often said it was his favourite night of the year. The band stayed out until well past midnight, finishing with the two carols he liked most – 'Brightest and Best' and 'Christians Awake, Salute the Happy Morn'. For me the greatest pleasure was to hear the band in the distance, its rich, warm sound floating over the roof-tops of the town. I would creep from my bed and sit by the window as the strains of 'The First Nowell', or 'God Rest Ye Merry, Gentlemen', came glowing through the dark. And then, in the morning, to stretch my legs down to the bottom of the bed to feel if my pillow-case was as full as I expected. Forgetting my indiscretions of other years I would rush into my parents' room shouting, 'He's been! He's been! Look at this ... and this ... and this ...'

After the presents had been opened we went downstairs for breakfast to discover a Christmas tree loaded with crackers, sugar mice, chocolate watches, gaudy baubles and fairy lights and, above the tinsel and candles, a fairy doll. It was always a real tree which father set in a bucket of earth and decorated with crepe paper. He always tried to buy a tree with roots in the hope of planting it in the garden ready for next year. 'You needn't bother', my grandfather would say. 'They boil the roots to make sure they'll not grow again.' And although father tried many times the tree soon died in our garden and seemed to be a fitting epilogue to our festivities.

As well as the tree there was a bran-tub – a wooden barrel filled with bran or straw in which were hidden several presents of small value. There was no greater sense of delight (or disappointment) than to plunge one's hand into the tub to see what we could find. It was always a mystery and not every parcel contained a gift. Sometimes one could pull out an empty box or an old sock wrapped in paper.

On Christmas morning we also found the sideboard heavily laden with bowls of oranges, nuts, dates, liquorice allsorts, and bottles of port wine – ruby, tawny and white. The room had been so transformed since we last saw it that it belonged to another world. The table was already laid for breakfast and, following tradition, we all sat down to a large home-made pork-pie beneath whose crust was rich meat and succulent jelly. A slice of that, with a round of brown bread and butter and plenty of mustard, got the day off to a good start and, in some ways, I saw breakfast as more important than Christmas dinner. Certainly the memory of it has lasted longer.

After breakfast, mother and father disappeared into the kitchen to continue preparations for dinner and we amused ourselves with our new toys. Once there was a wooden fortress with a drawbridge that worked on chains; once a tank which could climb over any obstacle, and once a rubber dagger whose blade slid back into the handle each time you stabbed someone. Once there was a regiment of hussars on shining black horses and once a cowboy's outfit complete with a gun. Why all these toys of aggression were chosen for me I don't know. Only once do I remember getting a painting-book or box of building bricks and I found both too elementary for my ambitions to create a masterpiece. Later, when father mistakenly saw me as an engineer, I had a Meccano set, but he spent more time playing with it than I did. On another occasion I received a fretwork set and was expected to produce the most complex patterns within minutes of taking it out of the box. The oddest gift I can recall, however, was the pair of boxing-gloves my younger brother John received when he was eight or nine. A gentle pacifist from the day he was born, it was unlikely that he would show any aspirations then for pugilism, any more than he would have seen himself as a scalp hunter when he was given a wooden axe carved with pride by my father who decided one year that a tomahawk was the most eagerly anticipated gift his second son required.

But Christmas was more than presents. Above us the ceiling was festooned with paper decorations, balloons and crackers. No one bothered how much coal or wood was put on the fire. The room just grew hotter and hotter. And, into this confusion of noise, colour and smells, my grandparents came to spend their Christmas quietly with us.

One year the decorations caught fire from one of the Chinese lanterns and all the balloons burst. There was a great fanning of arms and towels and stamping of feet. The room filled with a grey cloud of smoke that spread into a black snowstorm. I rushed out into the yard, shouting 'Fire! Fire!' But there was no one to hear me. The neighbours were all involved in their own fires. The forlorn white world outside looked cold and desolate. Only the birds had life as they pecked away at the few scraps which had been thrown out for them. The sky was as expressionless as a frozen pond. The wash-house looked faraway and deserted and, from the water-tap, hung a long icicle as gnarled and white as candle-wax.

When mother called me back into the house the panic was over. The smoke was disappearing through the open window and I could see quite clearly the unperturbed faces of the china dogs on the mantelpiece. From the ceiling hung the wire skeletons of the Chinese lanterns and the charred pieces of tape on which the balloons had once blossomed. Another drama was over all too soon.

For several years it was customary for my grandparents to spend their Christmas Day with us, either to stay all day or, after dinner, to go to my aunts for tea and the evening's entertainments. When they stayed all day with us it was usually expected that my aunts, uncles and cousins would come round to spend the evening with us as well. Then the fun was four-fold and the events unpredictable. The large round table that always stood in the centre of our front room, was cleared for cards, dominoes or 'tippit' (a game in which one team passed a coin from hand to hand, the hands always hidden beneath the table; the other team then had to guess which person held the coin when the clenched hands appeared on the table-top. One by one the hands were dismissed until the opponent thought that the coin-hand had been reached and would then declare 'TIPPET!' At which point the hand had to reveal whether or not it contained the coin.) While games went on at the table, the door to the stairs was closed to take the dart-board or hoopla, or blind man's donkey. We also played postman's knock, tiddly-winks, draughts, consequences, or hunt the thimble, or made up our own games from the costumes and props around us. There was singing and laughter as stories of local characters who haunted our Christmasses then like ghosts of long ago, were recalled. If half of those stories were true, no town ever knew more clowns, lunatics, drunks or eccentrics than Whittlesey. We heard of old farm-workers in the fens who were laws unto themselves – men who never washed from one year's end to another, who worked stripped to the waist even in winter, and who wrestled with bulls for shilling bets or drank a yard of ale at The Three Fishes before anyone could sing one verse of 'Little Brown Jug'. One uncle told a murder story gruesome beyond belief, while another sang 'Ten Green Bottles'. We heard about the days when the King's Dyke Silver Prize band went out carol-playing in snow so deep that they lost their euphonium player and, of how Flowery George tripped over his lantern and rolled into a ditch, shouting, 'Play on, boys! Play on!' The family laughed as it laughed each year as one story prompted another so that, by the end of the evening, everyone had recalled some favourite anecdote.

Many of the local characters had fascinating nicknames – Ducky Benstead (who was a wild-fowler), Porky Frost (who was a butcher), Clocky Norris (who was a watch repairer) and Buzzer Lovell (who sounded the work's hooter). There were other names that imprinted themselves on the memory for the deeds or sayings associated with them – Billy Cuckoo, Billy Blunt, Oliver Hailstone, Tassie Roberts, Sam Hilliam and Buckie Anderson – men who became legends and expressed something of that typical fenland independence that has made us, as Dr Bernard once said, 'a race apart.'

As children, we were always allowed to stay up late on Christmas Day to have supper with the rest of the family.

Despite all the good things we had received since early morning, we would have felt deprived had we not been allowed to share in that final feast of cold chicken, pressed tongue, home-cured ham, the remains of the pork-pie, and a variety of pickles which had been made during the summer and autumn months – pickled shallots, red cabbage and pickled walnuts, with a selection of chutneys and cheese – all too good to miss at eleven o'clock at night.

My uncles encouraged me to eat more than intended and,by their ribald teasing, enabled me to show-off without fear of retribution. Often some innocent remark or action of mine caused them to rock with laughter and I was not slow to take advantage of the situation. Once, when I was about three or four, my mother was preparing me for bed and washing me in the living-room in front of the fire. Although everyone had finished eating they still sat round the table talking and paying no attention to me at all. So I lifted up the little vest I was wearing and shouted, 'Look at my pickled walnut!' After a moment of shocked silence they all burst out laughing and I heard my mother chuckle behind her embarrassment. Mildly drunk with my success I was taken up to bed, wishing that Christmas could go on for ever. Admittedly, we still had Boxing Day to come but that never quite held the same magic for me then, any more than it does now. After Christmas Day now I wish we could take down all the trimmings and get back to normal.

It was a tradition for us in those pre-war days to go round to one of my aunts for the afternoon and evening and I enjoyed these opportunities of a little more freedom. There I could take part in more games with a host of cousins who chased each other up and down stairs, hid in cupboards, or raided the kitchen for whatever food was left. It was there where I first sampled my first dog-end of a cigar or took an extra swig from the port bottle, and where I first began to explore the anatomy of girls. There were always dark corners or bedrooms where we could hide for a few minutes before being discovered. 'Let me look' or 'Let me feel' were uttered with breathless anticipation before someone shouted from below, 'What are you up to up there?'

Walking home late at night with my parents through the familiar but darkened streets always gave me a tremendous pleasure of knowing where I belonged. There were still lights on in most of the houses and, beyond the blinds or curtains, were secret worlds which made me want to pry, to eavesdrop on those other people's lives. Most of the houses had no secrets in the daytime. I knew the people and their rooms. Their furniture would have been much like ours, their Christmas gatherings very similar. But the light beyond the blinds tempted speculation and I was intrigued.

By the time we reached our own dark house I was tired and ready for bed. Once again Christmas had lived up to its annual expectations and I was more or less ready for the days to return to their more familiar pattern and a swift approach to spring.

I think there was only one Christmas that did not make us happy and that was a year when my father had to work on Christmas Day. The brickyards had to be kept open, the kiln fires fed, and father's shift was doubled so that he worked a whole day and part of the night. Because he could not get home for Christmas dinner my grandparents did not come to us as usual and not all the decorations or trimmings could make up for this loss. I knew that mother was upset and neither she nor my sister could be persuaded to play games. Not even my new magic lantern made it feel like Christmas and, when I dropped one of the glass slides on the kitchen floor, my misery was complete. I picked up the pieces knowing it could never be repaired. The breakage summed up the misery of the day and I was grateful when I was told it was time for bed. Looking from my window at the other houses in the street, I resented all the fun that might still be going on in those rooms beyond the curtains and drawn blinds. I saw no reason why I should say my prayers until mother said, 'If your father had not gone to work today he wouldn't have a job next week, and you know what that would mean. If he doesn't have a job there'll be no holidays next year for you or any of us, will there?'

No holidays? I needed no more coaxing. I prayed fervently for all the right things, then went to sleep. By the time my grandparents came to tea the following Sunday I think my view of the world had been restored. Grandad sat puffing his pipe as I built him a house with my new set of bricks. Grandma sat regally putting the world to rights and complaining mildly that I should not be allowed to talk to myself so much. She was a very different character from grandfather. She was educated, liked books, read the Bible, and had once been organist at the Primitive Methodists' Chapel, where she also worked as a Sunday-school teacher. She spoke well, dressed well and always expressed her opinion as if she was the country's leading authority on any subject. Having completed her housework in the morning she always changed after lunch into something more ladylike – a black dress with lace, jewellery and a fox's fur. Sitting in our house she looked more like the family's own Queen Victoria holding court, ruling with a straight rod, a ready quotation from the scriptures, and a no-nonsense attitude to the world's wrongs. My father said he was never smacked by his father, a quiet word was enough. But, if that failed, his mother soon took over with her own method of discipline, which included a long thin cane or a leather strap. 'Spare the rod and spoil the child' was a dictum close to her heart and most of her grandchildren were to remain in awe of her at times, even though we loved her.

My grandparents' marriage puzzled me as I grew older because there were so many differences between them. Grandfather, gentle, patient, persuasive and unambitious; grandmother volatile, proud and strong-willed. Whatever she had been, or could have been before her marriage, her chosen role brought her down to a very ordinary, hard and simple life, one which I am sure she must have resented at times. With a large family to support she was often forced to spend her last few pence on a rabbit stew which, with some home-grown vegetables, had to supply the only meal that day for seven or eight hungry bellies. My father often said that he could not remember ever wearing an overcoat as a child. A grey woollen pullover was the only extra item of clothing he had for the snow when he walked to school with his slate under his arm. There was one pair of boots for weekdays and one for Sundays, which were polished and repaired until he finally grew out of them. As he was the youngest of the children there was no one left to have his cast-offs. Their chequered life had reached their end.

It was my grandmother's belief that the end of the world was imminent and she could not understand why people

wanted to bring children into this life where they would know
nothing but evil and suffering. 'I'm glad I had mine when I did,
Sarah', she would say to my mother. 'I would never want them
to come into this wicked world now', forgetting that four of
her offspring had died in the poverty and smog of London
where evils were a little more plentiful than in Whittlesey with
all its scandals. When the Second World War was declared she
nodded knowingly. 'What did I tell you? We are seeing the
latter days, you mark my word. I only hope the Good Lord will
have mercy on us and protect us. If the throne of England falls
it will be the end of the world.'

She was always forthright if not always rational in her
remarks and her pride made her reluctant to accept anything
which she thought was second-rate. The one thing which she
was not prepared to accept, or understand, was the system of
clothing-coupons which was introduced during the war. Nor
did she approve of the practice of having articles of clothing
or furniture, for which she had paid good money, stamped
with the word 'UTILITY'. She considered that as degrading
as the word 'PAUPER'. 'I've half a mind to write to Mr
Churchill about it and ask him how he'd liked to be stamped
all over with a word like "Utility".'

One of the clearest memories I have of her, and her old
rambling house in Whitmore Street, is of a day I spent there
when I was four. The King's Dyke Silver Prize Band had
qualified for the finals of the National Brass Band Contest,
held each year at the Crystal Palace, and several of the
bandsmen took their wives with them to make it 'a real day
out'. My mother, after much persuasion, agreed to go as well
that year, so my sister and I were taken round to stay with
grandma.

Her rooms were better and bigger than ours, each one full
of interesting objects and atmospheres. There was not an
empty cupboard or corner to be found. Glass domes of
stuffed birds stood on the sideboard, or on the chest of
drawers near the window, and on the mantelpiece beside the
clock were jars, ornaments and tins. There was a tea-caddy
full of sweets, and another full of coloured buttons. She had a
tray of mounted butterflies and a case full of photographs.
On the walls hung pictures of battlefields, with horses,

cannons and uniformed soldiers in various positions of dying. They might have been of the First World War or perhaps, more likely, the Crimean War. I can clearly remember being fascinated by those scenes of drama, with horses rearing in clouds of gunfire smoke and men impaled on bayonets. One of grandma's many boxes of memorabilia contained the pearl shirt-studs and cuff-links which had once belonged to a cavalry officer killed at Balaclava, so the pictures must have been of that conflict. When I became bored with these she threaded some wool through the holes of a large amber button so that I could spin it like a propeller as I worked my arms in and out as if playing a concertina.

I was asleep on the black leather couch in her living-room when, in the early hours of the morning, my parents arrived home and called to take us back to our own house in Church Street. I was too drowsy to hear or care whether my father's band had won or not. I was only half-conscious of being lifted up by him and carried home through the silent streets, the cool night air mixing with the smell of his uniform impregnated with tobacco-smoke and his stale body-heat. All I remember hearing my mother saying was 'I'll never leave them again, never ...' She told me years later that it was the most miserable day in her life and she never wanted to see London again.

My grandparents' house was also something of a mystery to me for it had, I believe, been left to grandma by a grateful benefactor. There was a stained-glass window on the landing which appealed to me, and a wide staircase with a bannister. The property also included a row of small cottages nearby which were let to tenants for a rent of one-and-sixpence a week. But, as few of them paid when they should, this source of income did not swell the domestic purse all that much and, when grandmother asked one of the tenants to quit because he had not paid any rent for over six months, he told her that she could keep her rotten old pigsty as he was looking for a cheaper place anyway. Another tenant was the father of twins and, when the babies died, he told her in all seriousness that he could only afford to go into mourning for one. 'One's hern and th'other's mine. I'll only go in mourning for mine. She can please 'erself.'

That house, like ours, has gone now and all that remains is a chestnut tree planted by my eldest aunt when she was a small girl ninety years ago. Each year, when the leaves fall, I see more ghosts in the air and glimpse beyond its bare branches the mirage of a ruined house where there were dreams now long-forgotten. When the house became uninhabitable and my grandparents too old to manage it, they moved with Aunt Daisy to a new house on Eastrea Road and their visits to us became less frequent. They still came to us at Christmas and we would often go to see them, but my memory of their last years is clouded by their illness and death, and a deep regret that I had not listened more to their own memories and conversations when I had had the chance.

After Christmas the calendar followed its predicted course of birthdays, Mothering Sunday, Good Friday and Easter, band concerts and harvest festivals. As grandfather would say, 'you can never get lost in the year for long.' In addition to the annual events there were occasionally political demonstrations or religious revivals – excuses for more parades and noise in the town and an ancient need in man to march.

The most sombre day of the year was undoubtedly Good Friday when only fishmongers and carpenters were expected to work. When I asked why, I was told that we should not eat meat on Good Friday because that was the day that Jesus was crucified and carpenters were made to work because they had been responsible for making the cross on which Christ had died. It all sounded very complicated and unfair and prompted one of my uncles to say to me one year, 'So if you want to make sure of an extra day's work when you grow up you know what you'll have to be.' From what I remembered of my Sunday School classes it was the Romans who had killed Christ, and how could we be sure that carpenters made all the crosses that were needed for crucifixions all those years ago? It became even more confusing when someone else tried to explain that it was really the Jews who had killed Jesus and the Romans were only carrying out orders. So, for whatever reason, we ate fish and hot-cross buns, and I waited for the sky to go black from twelve noon until three o'clock when the heavens would be rent asunder. They rarely were. The sun often shone on Good Friday as it might have done on any other spring day and I wondered what had gone wrong. There were several extra services we had to attend and sometimes a Passion play in the schoolroom in the evening where we hissed Judas and booed Barabbas, or wept with Mary Magdalene.

After the brooding drama of Good Friday there was only one more day to endure before we received the chocolate eggs that mother had hidden in one of the cupboards until Easter Sunday. There was no mistaking when that day arrived because at half-past six the Salvation Army band gathered outside its hall, further down the street, and then paraded through the town, playing and singing with sleep-shattering gusto —

> *Up from the grave He arose,*
> *With a mighty triumph o'er His foes.*
> *He arose a victor from the dark domain,*
> *And He lives for ever with His saints to reign.*
> *He arose! Hallelujah! Christ arose!*

Behind the band marched many of the members of the corps who were not bandsmen — women playing tambourines and rejoicing with enough enthusiasm to wake all the dead as well as the living, bringing down the walls of Jericho into the bargain. Their joy was without doubt very sincere and their intentions honourable but, for the men who had only just climbed into bed after working all night in the brickyards, such boisterous declarations of the unnatural were not always greeted with sympathy. My father, a man fully in agreement with their faith, groaned more than once as the beating drum made the window rattle and cornets slashed the gentle shades of dawn. Others, like him, turned over in their tired bones and postponed their resurrections until midday. They were at least charitable enough to laugh about the drummer who one year lost his way. He was so short that when the drum was strapped on to his chest he could not see which way the band went. To overcome that disability the bandmaster wrote out the route for him and pinned it to the rim of the drum. The only problem was, the drummer couldn't read so when the march was rearranged one year the band went one way and he went the other. To his dying day he claimed that the band had gone wrong and that he was the only one to finish the parade. That incident endeared him to the town even more than the brown boots he always wore with his uniform and, when he died, a fellow bandsman was heard to say, 'I wonder – which way did he go?'

Death was a much closer reality to a child before the post-war age of a Welfare State provided geriatric wards, or funeral parlours took charge of the body when all breath was spent. Before then most old people (and young for that matter) died at home in their beds and were cared for by members of the family who took it in turns to sit up with the patient through the night. When death was imminent the whole family was called to gather in the sickroom for the moment of departure. 'He's gone!' or 'She's gone!' were words as familiar as, 'No milk today, thank you.'

I remember visiting both my grandparents on the day they died and could smell death in the air. It was almost visible, a spectre in black waiting for its next victim. Once, when I was no more than seven or eight, I went with my father who had offered to sit by the bedside of his dying aunt. Why I was not left at home I do not recall. Perhaps my own mother was ill, or nursing one of her own children. I know it was late afternoon and getting dark. My great-aunt's room was packed with furniture, including a wash-stand on which stood a large china bowl and jug. My father frequently dipped a cloth into the bowl of water and patted his aunt's brow. Then she started to make a strange noise in her throat. 'What's she doing that for?' I asked. 'That's what's known as the death-rattle', my father explained. 'It won't be long now. You'd better run home and tell your mother.' Within an hour other members of the family arrived and stood in silence as the old lady's final breath fluttered from her lips and she 'was gone'. Later, a woman (who also served the town as a midwife) came to perform the washing and 'laying-out' and she was followed by the undertaker who arrived to measure the body for its coffin. The corpse stayed in the house until the day of the funeral – its nostrils stuffed with cotton-wool, its eyes closed yet still able to stare through you. Such familiarity with 'a death in the house' provided me with images for my writing more than forty years after the experience –

There was a reason once
for returning to these fields.
Even in winter their soil gave hints
of something called Spring.
Now they are laid out
like the corpse of an old man,
his nostrils stuffed with snow,
his veins stiff with ice ...

Today it is all much tidier and distant. The grief may not be lessened by the removal of the body to a funeral parlour or a chapel of rest but the oppressive presence of death in the house has been relieved. I see no point in wailing over a corpse. Only the life that was held within its shell is worth preserving. At such moments we simply take on another life to live.

7 Fag-cards by lamplight

What else happened in those years before 1939? The shoe-box is a bit short on photographs for the years 1937 and '38. The only ones of me show a small, toothless child grinning at the school photographer hidden under a large black cloth draped over his tripod. The crudely tinted print gave me unnaturally pink cheeks and bright blue eyes. The colours were more like those I achieved with my magic painting-book where I simply brushed clear water over the page and a picture appeared with hideous shades of green, red, yellow and blue.

The day I started school presents a more vivid picture. Because of my earlier illnesses I did not begin school until I was six and I can remember my mother taking me to the infants' school in Broad Street to commence my formal education. We walked solemnly down the street, through Thoroughfare Lane, with my mother reassuring me all the time that I was going to like school and make lots of new friends. I did not share her enthusiasm, did not want any more friends, and vowed I wouldn't stay. It did not help to be told that it was the same school to which she and my father had gone when they were little, nor that some of the teachers were the same ones who had taught them what little they knew.

The other children were already a year ahead of me and I resented their superiority. No one is better at intimidating a child than another child. A classful of them was awesome and, as I was the only new boy starting that morning, all their attention was focused on me.

'Who's 'e, Miss?'

'Wot's 'is name?'

'Where's 'e gonna sit?'

Familiar setting for the annual photograph, taken
probably for my fourth birthday - 1934.

Grandma and granddad Storey with my brother John, outside our house in 1937.

The first of many studio portraits of my sister Freda and me, 1931.

My parents on their wedding-day - 2 June 1923.

Mother, with the grandmother who brought her up in
Whittlesey, *c.*1920.

Mother - Sarah Ann Elmes - taken just before her marriage.

Father - Ernest Edward Storey - who was the youngest of twelve children, taken in 1922.

First school photograph, taken
at Broad Street Infants
School, Whittlesey in 1935.

The King's Dyke Silver Prize Band, with father and uncle third and fifth
on second row, 1935.

The Annual United Sunday School gathering on Whittlesey market-place, 1925.

Church Street as it would have been in 1930 - our house halfway down on the left.

One of the last family holidays we
had together before the Second
World War.

With my father and sister, standing in the sea at Heacham, 1933.

'Wot's 'e still got 'is cap on fer?'
'Why's 'e brought 'is mother?'
'Ain't 'e fat!'

Fen children were not timid, not even in the classroom, and their inquiries and observations seemed to go on for a long time before the teacher finally silenced them. Looking at those thirty-four faces was like waking in the middle of a nightmare. My boots were nailing me to the floor. I wanted to turn and run out of the room but could not move. My head throbbed, even though my mother had by now removed the cap, and I knew I was scarlet from embarrassment. I noticed the strange smells of the classroom – chalk, plasticine, milk, stale water in flower vases, and the children. I looked at the windows. They were high, and closed. I looked at the doors. There was the one through which I had come and another which led into a different classroom already full of other children. There was no escape. I knew then that I had lost those green fields and rivers for ever. When the headmistress had finished talking to my mother she handed me over to the class-teacher. My mother bent down to kiss me goodbye and gave me a banana to eat at playtime. The rest of the class laughed and, although I tried not to cry, I could not keep back the tears. In my anger I threw the banana across the room and attempted an escape. But the teacher had a firm hold of me and took me to a desk at the back of the room. And there I sat, staring out of the high windows of a Victorian school at the bright blue sky that had been stolen from me. Years later the teacher then responsible for me told me, 'You were the quietest child I ever had. You never asked a question, never answered a question, and you never even put up your hand to leave the room. You just sat staring out of the window all day and quickly earned yourself a name as 'the dreamer'.

I am grateful that she allowed me to do so much dreaming for I am sure my imagination was educated if not my brain. I do not believe, however, that I could have spent all my time sky-gazing because I can remember weaving raffia through cardboard rings, and counting little mottled cowrie shells. I also learned how to use plasticine, how to draw, make letters and read. I was even given the triangle to play in the percussion band and persuaded one morning to recite a poem about the moon. But little progress was made in the more important subjects. Arithmetic was so alien to my reasoning that to this day I still dread the task of adding two figures together and never question the amount of change I receive in a shop. The finer art of mathematics is a mysterious religion practised in a language I do not understand by an amazing number of people who are otherwise quite normal. I could memorize the Psalms better than I could the multiplication tables but that did not qualify me for leading in the weekly star-card parade. Each week every child's work was reviewed and coloured stars accorded for reading, writing, arithmetic and spelling. We all lined up, in order of merit, and on Friday afternoons were led into the Assembly Hall. Those with four stars headed the procession, followed by those with three, two and one. Those with none brought up the humiliated remnants of the class and were seen to be the dolts we probably were. I truly do not remember gaining many stars, though one of my teachers later assured me that I always fitted my writing 'so neatly into the lines on the page' that I must have been commended for that.

Although most of the children were known to me outside the school (even if they did not live in our street), there were some who were always to remain strangers. Their polite name was gypsies but we called them 'diddicoys'. Their personal names were much more fascinating – Eunice Hinny Thammagadd Hue Paora Chamberlain was one, and Queenie Elizabeth Harrington was another. There were plenty of Smiths and Grays and most of these families lived on their own camp-sites at the edge of town. The children were irregular attenders at school and we were not encouraged to be friendly with them. 'You'll bring enough head-lice home without mixing with that rough lot' said mother. And true enough, the steel lice-comb was pulled through my hair every Friday night before it was washed with disinfectant soap.

I continued to sit at the back of the class and shared a desk with a girl whose name was June. She was a waif-like creature with a generous nature. Immediately behind our desk was a radiator. One morning I carelessly leant back in my chair and rested my head on the hot metal, which burnt my neck. I started to cry and was convinced the injury was fatal. But little June came to the rescue by removing her knickers and wrapping them as a bandage round my neck. All was well. They were comforting and quickly charmed away the pain of any burns. When I returned to school after lunch I gave her a packet of pear-drops and we declared ourselves friends for ever. But when that year came to an end she went to a different school and I never saw her again.

By the end of the summer of 1937 I was old enough to be transferred to the junior school in Broad Street, which simply meant crossing the playground to another building. But it was a crossing I dreaded. It was like starting school all over again and I did not want to go. This was the first step away from childhood. It was where the other boys made a concerted effort to get me to swear. I knew what bad language was and had, once or twice in my temper, used a word for which I was punished, but we heard very little swearing at home and were told often enough never to use it. At Sunday School we were taught that even words like 'damn' and 'blast' were bad enough to get you sent to hell and anything stronger would be sure to get us sent to the hottest corner of that burning pit. So I took a pious stand on the matter when the boys in the playground tried to convert me. They gathered round me one day and said 'Bet you, Tubby Storey, you can't say this –

> *I'll chase that bug*
> *Around a tree,*
> *I'll have his blood,*
> *He knows I will.*

Falling for the bait, I replied, 'that's easy. Anyone can say that.'

'Go on, then, say it ... nice and slow.'

I did as they asked and responded to their applause.

'Now see how fast you can say it.'

Proud of my good memory and ability at reciting, I vainly accepted the challenge, declaring loudly – '*I'll chase that bugger round a tree. I'll have his bloody nose I will.*'

They all burst out laughing and went round telling all the girls that I was swearing like a trooper. The girls came to see if it was true and I had to repeat the verse to avoid further ridicule. But for the next few days I felt terribly guilty and afraid. Did this mean that I would really go to hell? As the weekend passed without any such retribution I gained confidence and my vocabulary was added to day by day in the playground so that I was soon using swear-words with ease. When I absent-mindedly announced at home one evening that I was 'just going outside for a piss' there was a deathly silence, then a snigger from my sister, and finally a shrug of the shoulders from my mother who had to admit that I was a normal boy after all. Even so I was given a lecture on the matter and told never to let her hear me use such words again. The lesson I learnt that night was that one needed just as good a memory in order to swear as one did to lie.

The only lesson I can remember enjoying in the junior school was music. I could already play the cornet, was having piano-lessons and loved singing. I could draw a stave of musical notation in both treble and bass clefs, and had a natural sense of rhythm. The school only had a percussion band and even then I had to fight with the rest of the class to get some cymbals, a drum, triangle or tambourine. One day I arrived at the box too late and there were no instruments of any kind left. Pouts of disappointment and sulky protestations finally caught the teacher's attention who, knowing of my limited talents, decided not to punish me but invited me instead to be the conductor that morning. My moment had arrived. She assembled the percussion band in front of me and handed me the baton. The moment I took it into my hands I felt a thrill of vocation surge through my body. This was my destiny. The baton was a natural extension of my arm and, although I knew nothing of orchestras then, that motley collection of percussion instruments before me became at least the Black Dyke Mills Band. I may have been the only one in the class who knew the difference between a crotchet and a minim and I was determined to make the most of it. Now I could get my own back on Bully Brown and Tiger Green. Now I could tell Peggy and Molly and Elsie and May who was really the boss. I could tell that spiteful girl on the triangle that she was out of tune. I could accuse the side-drummer of being tone-deaf. Harp-like arpeggios of power went up and down my spine as my arms flapped ungainly as I tried to keep the band in time with Miss Gunton at the piano. It was my only moment of glory. Next week I was back on the triangle.

The only other time that my musical talent allowed me to have such a feeling of power was a few years later when I was given the job of pumping the bellows for the chapel organ on Sundays. I volunteered for this job to get out of sitting still so long in the hard pew occupied by my parents. Then, one night, flagging towards the end of a very long hymn, I realized that I had the entire congregation at my mercy, not to mention the organist. If I were to stop pumping, the organ would soon wheeze to its final cough and the singing flounder. My nerve never allowed me to go that far but I did 'go slow' on a few occasions until the lady organist insisted that the task should be given to someone more responsible. It went to a cousin and I was back in the pew with my parents until they decided I was old enough to join the choir.

Although music took up much of my time I did not exclude myself from the other activities of the street or playground. I enjoyed playing fag-cards, marbles, cricket and conkers. I was no good at hop-scotch, whip-n-top, or hoops but, as these were mainly looked upon as girls' games, it did not worry me, nor was I too enthusiastic about football.

One of the favourite hobbies of boys then was collecting cigarette-cards and, as most of our fathers smoked, we soon had complete sets of boxers, footballers, sports cars, aeroplanes, badges or military uniforms. We competed for them, lied for them, paid and accepted bribes for them, and guarded them with a diligence afforded to possessions of great worth. More than once I slept with my latest collection under the pillow and was reluctant to use them in the street. More toecaps were worn out from kneeling on pavements to play fag-cards than ever football could claim. The streets were lined with combatants displaying a variety of skills. You could lose or win fifty cards a game. Wherever a wall and a smooth surface could be found, boys became engrossed in the art of flicking these small cards towards the 'jack' or covering their opponent's last throw. Matches went on until daylight failed and then continued under the yellow glow of one of the street's gas-lamps. We fretted over our losses as financiers do over their stocks and shares. Those cards which were not used for playing were collected into albums. Any spares were traded-in for others we may not have. 'I'll give you two Jimmy Wildes for one Tommy Farr ... ' or 'Who'll take a Joe Louis for a Freddie Mills?' The series of cards we did not mind losing were those of wild flowers, famous buildings or film stars.

My music suffered more in summer when there was no school and I could ride out into the fens on my bike and spend hours on my own. I always preferred my own company and could escape the street within minutes of leaving the house. Whittlesey, although a town, was far less urban in those days than it is now. Where the streets ended the countryside began. There was a definite boundary where the buildings came to an end and the fields took over. I only had to ride as far as the railway-gates at Blackbush, Ramsey Road or Station Road and the town was left behind. The world was then all farm-land, space, sky and stillness. There I could sit and watch lizards, frogs, herons, skylarks, beetles, grasshoppers, moles and pheasants getting on with their existence as if no one else in the world mattered. I could study a colony of ants going about its own life style with as much purpose as human beings in a city, or I could follow the course of eels as they made their way along fenland drains, or catch a glimpse of an otter. But I never saw what my grandfather told me he once saw when he was working in the fens – a whole haystack on the move. When I asked him how that could happen he said, 'It was full of rats, boy, that's why. When a colony of rats decides to move that's a sight to frighten a man out of his wits.' He was having his 'dockey' at the time and said there were hundreds of rats in the stack. 'When the leader gave the signal to go, they all followed and the stack went with 'em until it collapsed on the other side of the road like a building collapsing in an earthquake.' I asked him if rats really had leaders and he assured me they did. 'All birds and animals do. You watch the starlings at twilight. When they do their sun-dance there's always one that starts 'em off. Same with martins and swallows when they're ready to leave. Same with eels.' I listened wide-eyed to all his stories and learned from him how to imitate the croak of a pheasant by blowing on a blade of grass held between my thumbs. Two things he possessed, and which I always wanted, were a penknife with a very sharp blade and a burning-glass, but he said I was too young for either. 'One can spill blood, the other cause fire.' But he often showed me how efficient they were by cutting tobacco with the knife and igniting it with the burning-glass.

The knife was eventually given to my father and I used to watch him sharpening it in the kitchen. I was reminded of this when clearing out the house after his death and I found the handle in an Oxo tin where he kept nails and screws.

> 'How sharp is it now?' I'd ask
> when he had honed the knife-blade
> on a pumice-stone kept for that
> purpose in the kitchen drawer.
>
> Stretching his forearm out, he'd cut
> a swath clean through the growth of hair
> like someone cutting corn, then say
> 'It's sharp enough, I think, you try.'
>
> I'd lightly draw the knife along his arm
> afraid that I might cut too deep and hurt.
> But it was not his flesh that bled,
> and only now I feel the wound.

One thing I did learn on those excursions into the fens was that when one of Nature's dramas appeared on our stage it came as a colossus striding across the earth determined to inspire awe, whether it came in the form of floods, blizzards, sunsets or fen-blows. If a full moon rising over the fens could fill me with wonder so too could a fen sunset setting fire to the sky beyond the fender of brickyard chimneys. There was nothing to hold it in. It spread along the earth's boundary in extravagant daubs of crimson, gold, orange and navy-blue, a raging furnace of colour in slow motion that reverberated throughout the rest of the sky so that even those clouds in the east were tinged pink by its fury. On such a vast scale everything was gigantic. When rivers burst their banks thousands of acres of land became water. When there was a blizzard it swept like a frightening war-machine across the fens, crushing telegraph-poles as if they were no more than matchsticks and ripping off the roofs of farm buildings as if they were made of paper. But one drama I had not been prepared for was a fen-blow. This is mostly a spring phenomenon when the land is drying out after winter and has just been sown with an early crop like sugar beet or carrots. The fine peat soil becomes very powdery and if a strong March wind begins to blow it can plane the top-soil off and swirl it into huge black clouds that darken the sky. It is like being in a black sand-storm. I had already found it too exhausting to bike in such a strong wind and stood looking across the fields of Black Bush when a distant howl from the west lifted tons of soil, seed and fertilizer into the air and swept it towards me. I crouched by a gate and heard the wind growing fierce. Strips of a nearby hedge were torn away and blown into the air. The sky was closer to midnight and I was afraid. The fine particles of soil were biting into my hands as I tried to protect my face. I thought that my grandmother's prophecy about the world coming to an end was about to come true. Earth was falling apart, being blown to pieces. There would be no more light, no more sun, no more going home. The storm lasted nearly an hour and when I was able to move I saw the narrow dykes around me were full of the soil which had been deposited by the wind from farms ten miles away. I was to experience many more – and sometimes worse – fen-blows but that day made me aware of how insignificant we can be made to feel when exposed to the elements in such a wild place.

I was now becoming increasingly inquisitive about some of the place-names in and around the town. King's Delph, I was told, was named after King Cnut, or Canute. But what of Beggar's Bridge, Burnt House Fen, Bassenhally and Briggate? Some of these names were already corruptions of earlier names. Bassenhally was once just Basinhall, Stonald Road was once Stoney Fold, and Drybread Road was the name given to the road which once led to the workhouse. One road, whose origins I did not know as a boy, was Scaldgate. *Scald*, or *Skald*, is a Scandinavian word for poet. So was this road in Whittlesey meant to be the gate of a poet? But which poet? What sagas might have been written or sung there centuries ago?

All these names are reminders of the other people who had once settled in the town and were to whet my later appetite for history but, as a boy discovering these places for myself, I could think of no one ever being there before me. The town was mine, and the fields were mine.

As summer gave way to autumn there were the usual tasks of picking blackberries and elderberries for our tarts or wine-making. The land around Whittlesey is not good blackberrying country so we had to search for them and they were often too sour to eat on their own. Most of what we picked went into the making of blackberry vinegar which we sprinkled on our puddings. The elderberries also went into cooking or the making of wine. Elderberry wine and parsnip wine were favourite products of working-class people, as was bee-wine, – a heady kind of mead made from pellets of yeast, sugar, warm water and flavouring. The large jars which were used for this preparation were usually placed on window-sills to catch the warmth of the sun. It was then that the "bees" began to work, going up and down in a silent buzzing which fascinated us as children. The mixture had to be fed with sugar once a week and, four or five weeks later, was then bottled. Some bottles were laid down for several years before they were drunk and were very potent by the time the cork was drawn. One family in our street kept some home-made wine for thirty-two years ready to celebrate their Ruby Wedding anniversary but, as the day approached, the wife suddenly became a staunch member of a temperance society and poured the lot down the drain. Their marriage was never the same after that, so I'm told.

No sooner were the hedgerows stripped of their summer fruit than we had to prepare for winter. The wash-house was stacked with wood, the cupboard under the stairs was filled with jars of chutneys, pickled shallots, cabbage and cooking apples. Winter had a spicy tang to it that filled the house with a promise of good meals to come. We take so much for granted now. We fill the freezer and nip down to the supermarket for anything we might have forgotten, but years ago there had to be a considerable amount of preparation for each season, especially winter. Hams were salted, shelves stacked high with whatever could be preserved; eiderdowns were refilled and blankets washed.

There were several things in winter's favour. If we had snow our lessons were usually interrupted by organized snowball fights in the playground. Old broken desks formed barricades and the classes were divided into two sides. We amassed our arsenal of white hand-grenades and then responded aggressively to the partisan encouragements of the teachers. After the battles we made long slides on the frozen snow and propelled ourselves at great speed towards the lavatory wall.

Winter sports extended beyond the school playground, especially if there had been several nights of severe frost. Before the Second World War all the fields on Whittlesey Wash were naturally flooded in winter and, with a few sharp frosts, these provided us with an enormous skating rink. Excess water from the River Nene and Morton's Leam used to overflow the banks and spread like an incoming tide up to the gas-works at the edge of town. Both sides of the road would be under water and the road itself disappeared beneath the flood. We only knew where it was by the rows of willow trees that lined its sides.

The fens have always enjoyed a reputation for producing fine skaters, many of whom earned a fame almost equal with that of well-known footballers. People still spoke of the Smarts, the Tebbutts, the Smiths and the Slaters in tones of awe. They had become legends. In 1895 Charles Tebbutt had skated a round trip of eighty-three miles in just over nine hours. In 1937 this was still a record. But distance was not the aim. It was speed that mattered. Fen skaters, with their peculiar stance of bending over almost at right angles with one arm behind the back, moved with the grace and swiftness of gazelles. Men came from as far away as Norway and Holland to compete with them.

It was not all competitive skating. When winter's grip was so firmly on the land, hundreds of people with nothing else to do gathered on the ice for a day's sport. Some would make a shilling or two sweeping the course where the local races were to be held. My grandfather did this on many occasions and also took a chair with him which he hired out to the gentry at twopence a time so that they had somewhere to sit while fixing their skates on to their boots. Before the sophisticated skating-boots were introduced from Norway most local blacksmiths were employed to make skates which could be strapped on to ordinary boots. Whittlesey people naturally believed there was nothing to beat 'Whittlesey

Runners' with their long sharp blades, but similar claims were made for those forged at Ramsey, March or Chatteris. Locally-made skates had been popular for more than a hundred years and some can still be found hanging in old barns or fenland museums.

The ice also provided fun for the children, whether we had skates or not. Sometimes we were given days off from school and spent much of this free time out on the arctic wastes playing with our hastily made toboggans. It was a Brueghel painting come to life, clusters of woollen-clad human beings dwarfed by the vastness of that white landscape. There men could forget for an hour or two that they were out of work. There the farmers forgot for a day that they were the bosses. Butchers and bakers gave joints of meat and loaves of bread as prizes. Skating became the leveller and many men kept their families alive during January and February by what they won on the ice. Some of these events became known as 'the Bread and Meat Races' and attracted a lot of entries, giving the day the air of a carnival.

There were times too when women took baskets of hot jacket potatoes and flasks of tea (occasionally laced with rum) which they distributed among the men. Sometimes, when the ice was particularly thick, Tom Blake drove his fish-and-chip van out into the middle of the arena and fried for most of the day. With black smoke oozing from the van's narrow chimney it looked more like an old tramp-steamer gone aground at the North Pole.

My father, who loved skating, often spoke of those nights when he skated until after midnight under a full moon, when the smooth ice glistened like silver and the only sound was the swish of the blades through the crystal frost. It was a love he inherited from his mother who, more than once, skated from Whittlesey to Peterborough and back to do some shopping.

Although we never get such an expanse of water now I still like to stand at the Dog-in-a-Doublet public house and look across the scenes that exist more in my imagination than in reality. Voices carry more clearly over the ice. Whispers are amplified by the darkening shadows. The past speaks out of the mist. Family likenesses are imprinted on the life-lines of sleep. We live in memory, in an unending quest for the links that are missing, or are now buried too deep in the soil. The landscape is a mirror which time has breathed on, hiding it perhaps for our own protection. But there are times when I wish to rub my hand over the glass, to peer through the mist in the hope of seeing something on the other side.

So, standing alone at the edge of a winter field, I try to remember, or rather imagine, those ancestors who once signed the ice with their passing. With what melodies did they rock the child's cot, or comfort their hearth-stones? What tunes did they learn from the wind's gut to lessen their grief, or lend dignity to their dead? To what music did they dance? With what rhythm did they welcome the spring or give praise for harvest?

I have stood so many times at the foot of this death-bed of winter that one day I might hear an answer to these perpetual questions. Some unborn summer will melt the unyielding earth and I shall be closer than I think.

> Beneath the soil,
> skin-deep for this day's measurement,
> remains the memory of a sea
> long before boundaries or shores
> decided who should plunder or betray.
>
> Beneath that sea
> from which our world was built
> there was the ice that separated land
> from land and bred a chasm in the bed
> of more than rock or tribe.
>
> Beneath the ice
> there was a fire which raged all winter
> in the bone proving there was a man ...

8 War-games near the workhouse

By 1938 there was a new prosperity coming into the lives of many ordinary people. Newspapers and the wireless were already talking of another war. Factories switched to making tanks, shells, rifles, lorries and uniforms for the services. Labour was again in demand. Runways were needed for new airfields. Wages improved and men soon found that they not only had jobs but could do overtime as well. Sunday work and double time became popular. Women were also needed in the factories, or for those jobs on the land being vacated by the men. Whatever was happening on the Continent, families were able to enjoy themselves in England more than they had been able to for years. Holidays were not only possible now but essential. My father, who had a year earlier lost his job in the brickyards, now had a job with a construction firm building runways. It meant cycling several miles to work each day but the pay was better and he was hoping to get into one of the work-gangs nearer home. As it happened he eventually got a job in one of the factories near Peterborough, where he became a machine-operator.

For our last family holiday together my father decided the following year to take us to Clacton-on-Sea. It was not as easy to get by train to this Essex resort as it was to Hunstanton or Cromer, so we asked our grocer, Mr Ashby, if he would take us by car if we paid for the petrol. In fact I think it would be truer to say that he first made the suggestion and we were happy to accept. So, one Saturday morning in July we all squeezed into his Standard 8. Father sat in front with my brother John on his knee; mother, sister and me – plus a large suit-case – were packed into the back, and off we went while our neighbours waved from open doors or peered from behind curtains until we were out of sight.

I never knew there were so many towns in England, with houses, pubs, shops and village greens. A new world was opening before me. But, squashed as I was in the back of the car, my legs began to ache and I started to ask, 'When are we going to get there? If we don't hurry up there won't be any seaside left.' My father turned and glared at me. 'Another word from you, my lad, and you'll go straight back home, so hold your tongue.' I knew this was an idle threat for how could I be sent home without all the others having to go home as well? Besides, it was Mr Ashby who had once asked me if I'd lost my tongue and he encouraged me to use it again by asking questions, such as, 'How many miles do you think we have travelled so far?' or 'How fast do you think we're going now?' or 'Count how many pubs there are called The Royal Oak before we get to Clacton.' But these questions were only a minor distraction and I was very grateful when we saw in the distance that shimmering horizon which was the sea.

Although I was now nine years old and more worldly wise since going to the junior school, Clacton surpassed my expectations. It was much bigger than any other seaside resort to which I had been. The sea was nearer, the pier longer, the amusements more exciting, and I was now tall enough to see *What the Butler Saw*. Deck-chairs were spread out along the sand like packs of playing-cards, as if the sun itself was playing patience. Boatmen called out their trips to far horizons in boats named *Mabel*, *Gertrude* or *Penelope*. One notice-board said *TAKE A PEEK AT EUROPE WHILE YOU CAN!* A man, pretending to be Tarzan, dived from the end of the pier and disappeared for seconds, while we all held our breath. There were Beach-time talent competitions, which I entered and sometimes won, and the girls wore briefer swimsuits than any I had ever set eyes on. Hot-air balloons floated like huge coloured moons in the sky. There were band concerts in the Pleasure Gardens, circuses on the pier, and we were allowed to stay up late to watch the firework displays. Abyssinia, Czechoslovakia and Poland were still mostly names in the newspapers. For a whole week I played upon the beach, made sand-castles and pyramids, or caught tiny crabs in pools of light. I watched the

Punch-and-Judy shows or strolled along the promenade for another ice-cream or stick of lettered rock. A man took more photographs of us, another (who was blind) made sculptures out of sand, only to be ruined by the next high tide, and the sun shone ... I could have stayed forever until we stood the following Saturday morning outside the boarding-house, waiting for Mr Ashby to come and take us home. When that moment of departure came I wanted to get back as soon as possible. I had suddenly had enough of donkeys, cockles and swimsuits. I wanted the normality of our street, the familiarity of sounds and smells that would never go out with the tide. 'How long will it take?' I asked. 'Soon enough', said father, more to himself than me.

A few weeks later I went back to school and the few snapshots of our last holiday together were put into the shoe-box with all the others. And then it was Sunday 3 September 1939.

The promise of peace brought back from Munich by Mr Neville Chamberlain proved to be no more than the piece of paper he had waved at press photographers. Many people believed, far more than Chamberlain, that war would come and preparations were already being made. Air-raid shelters, sandbags and sirens were no longer the symbols of panic or eccentricity. Men were now volunteering for the armed services, women were taking jobs in the munition factories, and those who were too old to fight were offering their services in some branch of civil defence.

By the Saturday evening of 2 September, the country was anxiously waiting for the important announcement which the Prime Minister was to broadcast to the nation the following morning if no reply had been received from Adolf Hitler.

It was a warm, bright, early autumn day. The church bells had been ringing for the morning service – which would be the last time they would ring for a few years – and I desperately wanted to go out for a bike ride. My father and some of the neighbours stood outside their back doors talking about the seriousness of the moment. They had all been listening to the radio and knew we were poised between an uncertain peace and a possible disaster. The last few minutes ticked slowly towards eleven o'clock and the expiry of Britain's ultimatum to Germany. St Mary's clock struck the hour, followed by St Andrew's, and everyone went into their houses to switch on the radio. By eleven-fifteen the street was deserted, the town silent. The air was charged with a fierce foreboding. I stood shaking, more with excitement perhaps than fear, for I knew nothing of what war meant. Then the dry, metallic voice of Neville Chamberlain pierced eerily into our presence. His peace mission had failed. We were at war.

I can remember one of our neighbours suggesting that it was probably a good idea to have a drink and he went indoors to get a bottle of sherry and some glasses. 'It may be the last one we shall have together, Ernie', he said to my father, who was looking very depressed.

My first awareness of the war affecting our lives came with the arrival of the evacuees from London. The very word *evacuees* was ugly and chilling. Only officialdom could have chosen a word so soulless for people who were now homeless statistics.

Those who came to Whittlesey that following Sunday morning were, no doubt, as bewildered as all the others who went to Devon or Wales. They had been dispatched to us to be kept safe and out of Hitler's way for the duration of the war. Some, who stayed and never went back, can remember that moment more clearly than anything else. 'I was more scared of all that space and sky than I was of any old bombs', said one. 'It was so quiet and empty that it gave me a headache. I kept wondering where all the buildings were.' Another said, 'I was more frightened of the people sorting us out for our new homes. I couldn't understand a word they said.'

The evacuees were fetched from the station in cars and buses and then taken to our junior school, which was used as a reception centre. Many of the children were crying and already pleading to go home. Clutching their few belongings and gas-masks, they were put into various categories, depending on age, families, size and sex. Each child had an identity label tied to its clothes. Crowded together in utter confusion, they looked like victims of some awful indignity for which no one had yet thought of a name. They were children, yet not children. They stood as frightened creatures not knowing who they were, where they were, or what was happening to them. Some, out of fear, or desperation, could no longer control themselves and stood in a pool of piddle, which put them even lower on the list. The local women eyed them up and down and whispered dark comments among themselves –

'They could all do with a wash.'

'I hope I don't get that one, or her.'

'The kids'll be no problem but just look at some of the mothers.'

'Bless their little hearts', said a woman who already had five children of her own. 'I wouldn't want this to happen to any of mine.'

Gradually the evacuees were allocated to their new guardians but even the kindest words uttered in coarse tenderness must have sounded like death threats to them. 'Don't you be frit of us, boy. Yew'll be alright as soon as we git yew 'um!'

A large, fat man who kept a smallholding on the edge of town put his arm round two brothers. 'Come on. Just yew git into that car over there the pair on yer and stop blabbering. Yew'll soon git used to us. We're a bloody sight better than them old Jerry bombs what might be dropping on London, yew mark my words.'

The two boys climbed into the Ford van and were driven away to a house surrounded by fields, barns and animals. They were to stay there for the next four years and loved mucking-out the pigs and loading-up the van with crates of celery or cabbages for market.

After the first few weeks of being away from their native surrounding of London's suburbs, many of the children began to enjoy the freedom of the countryside and the intimacy of small-town life. Some, with Cockney wit and cunning, soon knew as much about the place as we did and introduced a slicker brand of bargaining into the playground. The fact that they doubled the sizes of our classes and made teaching virtually impossible, was seen by us as a blessing. There were problems, of course, and fights in the playground became more frequent and aggressive. Not all the evacuees who came to Whittlesey were happy and, when the air-raids did not materialize as soon as expected, quite a lot of the children went back to their mothers, only to be killed a few months later when the bombs began to make London a city of ruins.

Although we were never blitzed we did have some scares and always expected the worst. Each night when the air-raid siren sounded we hurried from our beds, went downstairs to sit in the cold semi-dark room, and waited for something to happen. It became a habit for my father and the neighbours to stand outside on the garden path, speculating on which city was being attacked that night. Sometimes I was allowed to join them. With a mixture of fear and excitement I watched the searchlights probing the sky for German bombers which could be heard throbbing in the night sky as they made their way to the Midlands – Birmingham or Coventry. Their engines had a peculiar, syncopated rhythm that pulsated like a monster's heart-beat. The sound was unmistakable. Sometimes the gun-batteries around the town opened fire and the air trembled. But little else worried us. The noise of the planes receded. The searchlights drained from the sky. The All Clear whined over the roof-tops and we went back to bed. We only knew what might have happened to someone else when we saw the heavily censored pictures and reports in the newspapers, or listened to the radio.

Highly exaggerated accounts were received from the propaganda broadcasts of Lord Haw Haw, who became something of a cult as millions of people tuned-in each night to hear Germany's version of the war being read by this Irish-American traitor with a phoney English accent. His only rival – for a very different reason – was Tommy Handley with his radio-programme *ITMA* (It's That Man Again). His accent was genuine and the topical sketches of his shows were witty and morale boosting. His scriptwriters introduced into wartime entertainment some comic characters of an almost Dickensian stature.

Although the war appeared to be happening somewhere else we still got up each night when the siren went, just in case. Pots of tea were made, children played games under the table, often going into each others' houses for that pleasure, and once again the searchlights scissored the sky in the hope of picking up an enemy aircraft. Now and again a stray bomb dropped harmlessly in a field, or a damaged plane crashed on its way back across the fens, but we were never the intended target. The nearest direct raid was on the railway marshalling yard at March and a few bombs fell on Peterborough, but we knew nothing of the devastation inflicted on other towns.

If the night's alert lasted very long we were told by our teachers the following morning to fold our arms on our desks, rest our heads on our hands and try to sleep, to make up for our disturbed slumber. Even those children who had not bothered to get up for the air-raid took advantage of this time-wasting. These were the hours that many of us could have done with later when we discovered how little we had learnt during those vital years of our school lives. I hated these enforced rests. In such a cramped position I could hardly breathe and resented the time spent inhaling the stale smell of greasy desk-tops and blue-black ink. Even when we should have been working the teachers often arranged mock air-raids so that we could get in some practice runs to the shelters, which were several minutes from the school. On one occasion I was chastised for leaving my gas-mask behind in our classroom and was made to go back for it. I protested, explaining to my teacher that she was taking a double risk with my life for, if it had been a real air-raid, I stood as much chance of being bombed or machine-gunned as gassed. But it was no use. I had to return to the school to collect my mask. When I got back to the shelter I stood outside and listened to the rest of the class trying to sing *ALL THINGS BRIGHT AND BEAUTIFUL* through their bizarre headgear and I could not control my laughter. The teacher was convinced that I had become a victim of some new chemical warfare about which she had not been told.

Among the evacuees who joined our class was a boy called Danny who stood out from the rest of us because of his darker skin and skullcap. We couldn't understand why he always had to leave the room during assembly or morning prayers until, one day, Terry Street – a boy from Bethnal Green – took us aside. 'You lot know nuffin' do yer! It's because he's a Jew-boy, 'n it! He aint allowed to worship wiv us 'cus it was 'is lot what killed Jesus Christ, wannit! That's how *we* became Christians in the first place and why Danny can't say prayers wiv us.' Then he lowered his voice and looked very serious. 'That's why we should all hate the Jews and support Oswald Mosley.'

We didn't know who Oswald Mosley was and a few years were to pass before we saw the first grim pictures of the concentration camps. We were, at the time, being taught much more enthusiastically to hate the Germans. When a Messerschmitt was brought down just outside the town it was moved to a local garage in Eastgate and, as part of our war-time education, we were marched off to gloat over this small specimen of the mighty *Luftwaffe*. One by one we were lifted up and allowed to sit in the cockpit and were then shown the airman's helmet riddled with bullet-holes and stained with blood. Some of the boys put the helmet on and turned on the rest of us with mock machine-gun fire. The teacher smiled and said that until all the German pilots were shot down the war would not end. Although we were only ten or eleven years old we might well have to become pilots ourselves one day to shoot the enemy out of the sky or bomb German cities to free the world of their evil forever. Fired with such a mission we dreamt and talked for days of Spitfires, Hurricanes, Wellington and Lancaster bombers.

Most of our lessons were directed towards the war effort. Propaganda had subtle ways of preparing the next generation to hate the Germans. We painted posters for Victory, grew carrots for Victory, sang hymns and said prayers for Victory. We wrote essays, saved waste paper, collected silver paper and metal bottle-tops for Victory and promised so much of our pocket-money for National Savings Stamps so that the country had enough money for Victory. Even our history lessons were always about Victory. We had a tradition to keep, a cause to uphold. 'Think of Nelson', said our teacher, 'and the Duke of Wellington. Think of our own local hero, Sir Harry Smith, the hero of Aliwal who fought with Clive in India.' We knew there was a pub down Station Road called 'The Hero of Aliwal' but we had no idea who Harry or Clive were. We had to wait until we went to the Senior Boys School before we learnt about those men. 'But', said our school-teacher, 'men like that made England great and the next hero might well be sitting here in this school. Think of that. It could be you, or you …' There was a moment's silence as each boy examined his likely destiny but not one of us saw himself called towards such an illustrious place in history.

Nevertheless, the indoctrination went on. Art lessons were

no longer studies of plants or fruit but patriotic slogans and posters. 'Dig for Victory', and 'Look Out There's a Spy About' were on every hoarding and the devil now had a new name – 'FRITZ!' In our drawings of him we gave him clawed feet, a dragon's tail and fire spurting from his nostrils. Hitler was also portrayed in similar fiendish attitudes, sometimes as a vampire, sometimes as a pig, but he was always identifiable by his moustache. One of the most popular songs in the playground then was based on the music-hall song 'Run Rabbit Run', to which we put our own words –

> *Run, Hitler run, Hitler run, run, run.*
> *We're not afraid of the Hun, Hun, Hun.*
> *You'll get past with a bullet up your arse,*
> *So run, Hitler run, Hitler run, run, run.*

Our gardening lessons were held on the school allotments which were on the site of the old workhouse. This had recently been demolished with the help of a local tug-of-war team who used the tall chimney-stacks for training purposes. Their ropes would be tied to the chimneys and they would heave and strain in an effort to pull them down, which they eventually did. It was a good preparation for some of the national competitions they were to enter and they often beat some of the best teams in the country. The workhouse had always looked a bleak, forbidding place and my parents told depressing stories of people they had known who had been forced to spend their last days there. There was no accommodation for married couples so, after a lifetime together, old people were separated for their final years, the men being sent to one wing, the women to another. Looking through some of the registers I was surprised to see how many of our citizens passed through those doors. Some left of their own accord to take their chances 'on the road'; some were dismissed because of bad behaviour, and the rest died there and left in a pauper's coffin. Against one man's name was written 'Dismissed and Dead' presumably in that order. There was always a belief when I was a boy that Dickens had based his workhouse in *Oliver Twist* on Whittlesey's workhouse, but I supposed this could be claimed by a thousand other towns. He did visit Whittlesey on one or two occasions to see some acquaintances – two bachelor brothers by the name of Martin – and it is possible he saw our workhouse. Beyond that we have no proof. He would, no doubt, have found our town as depressing as he found Peterborough which, he said, 'is like the back door to some other place. It is the deadest and most utterly inert town in the British Dominion.' That did not prevent him from giving some of his famous readings in the city in 1855.

The Sir Harry Smith Community College now stands where that workhouse once stood and we grew radishes for victory. Drybread Road is no longer the pauper's route to final humiliation but a road of comfortable modern houses and, for all I know, the ghosts of the old building are all laid, if not forgotten.

With several searchlight and ack-ack units round the town we had an influx of soldiers who, thought some local people, needed entertaining. So, on Sunday evenings our chapel schoolroom was open for the troops to come and have a cup of tea and some refreshments. Afterwards we put on a short concert for them – a few musical items, a sketch or two, some community singing and a master of ceremonies who ceased to be funny the moment he tried to become a comedian. His opening remarks were always – 'Good evening, ladies and gentlemen, especially those in uniform. Before I speak, I would just like to say a few words ...' His cherry-red nose was not something put on for the occasion. It was a natural part of his jovial face. His humour was contagious and we laughed, whether he was funny or not.

Another local entertainer was Mr Popely who was an amateur magician when he was not being a postman. As boys we were eager to find out how each trick was done and waited for them to go wrong. 'Don't watch my hands', he'd say, 'watch my lips.' We did as we were told and the patter continued until the trick was safely completed without our noticing any sleight-of-hand. Sometimes the tricks did go wrong and no amount of hocus-pocus or wand-waving could put them right. We laughed and clapped as he became entangled in a labyrinth of Chinese rings or a mountain of silk handkerchiefs. The one trick he always got right was the one where he swallowed a length of string and spat out three ping-pong balls. Sometimes he told jokes and always explained that the reason why he never included 'sawing the lady in half' in his act was because the last time he did so the lady ended up a schizophrenic.

After Mr Popely came Joan, the 'Whittlesey Nightingale', who sang 'Bless This House' and 'The Holy City' to an accompaniment of rattling cups and saucers. As an encore she chose something lighter, such as 'There'll be Bluebirds Over', or 'Keep Smiling Through' so that the soldiers could join in the choruses. She became our own Vera Lynn rather than Jenny Wren and I was full of admiration for her then. She was older than most of the girls I knew, more attractive, and wore make-up – something frowned upon by some of the older women.

When all the sticky buns, rock-cakes and meat-paste sandwiches had been devoured, the audience sang 'Abide With Me' and we all went home. Some of the soldiers who came to the concerts also attended the chapel services first and became friendly with members of the congregation. My parents enjoyed inviting two or three home for supper and our Sunday-night fry-ups were a feature of the war. Everything that was left from Sunday lunch – potatoes, peas, cabbage, parsnips, remnants of mutton or pork, went into a large black pan which soon sizzled on the old gas stove while mother laid the table. Father was always cook and liked things well done, so the potatoes often came out crispy if not burnt. Sometimes we were able to get a few sausages which helped to make the meal even more substantial. Food-rationing tested everyone's ingenuity or skill in bartering. Ration-books were as precious as passports. Butter, cheese, sugar and meat exchanged hands for all kinds of favours. Brown-paper parcels slipped from overcoat pockets to shopping-bags. Clothes-coupons were swapped for cigarettes. The war made deception legitimate and several children illegitimate. Survival was paramount. Having something more than anyone else a common ambition. The only items we missed as children were sweets and chocolates. Otherwise our diet was plain but wholesome and for many Sunday evenings my father continued to provide gargantuan suppers of bubble-and-squeak or bangers-and-mash for our guests from the camp.

There was one moment he looked forward to, almost as

much as cooking the meal, and that was the entertainment afterwards in the front room. One of the soldiers, whose name was Trevor, was a good pianist and came from South Wales. To begin with he was no friend of mine for he could make our piano do things I couldn't. It was an old, ugly, stubborn instrument with brass candlesticks and a fretwork front. Its keys were as yellow as an old mare's teeth and I could hardly reach the pedals, which stuck when I did. If the piano had a mellow tone or could respond to a delicate touch, I had not found it. I was having lessons with a teacher in Gracious Street who used to provide the music in the local cinema during the silent-film era – not too long past in Whittlesey. Mr Lock was a kind of poor man's Paderewski, with long slender fingers and a sharp profile. He looked like a pianist and had taught some of his pupils to a commendable standard. What lost opportunity had condemned him to pounding out chase-music for westerns, or tear-jerking melodies for love stories, I do not know. Whether that was any better or worse than trying to teach boys like me is something I cannot answer. Week after week I went round to his house for my ninepenny lessons and did my best to please him. He was a patient man who wore a pin-striped suit and gold-rimmed spectacles. The fact that he never managed to get me beyond a hurly-burly piece called 'Fire! Fire!' might explain why he failed to become a household name, on the other hand I was probably unteachable for, at the end of that year, Mr Lock suggested that, as there was little improvement in my playing, my father would be wiser to save the ninepences and make me concentrate on my cornet-playing. It was only later that I came to love the piano as an instrument and taught myself to play Beethoven, Mozart and Chopin. In the meantime my renderings of 'Fire! Fire!' caused my parents many moments of anguish and despair. I used to blame the piano, of course, until this Welsh wizard arrived in khaki and transformed the eight-octave beast into a concert grand. Hardly a Sunday evening went by without him giving flawless performances of Ketelby's 'In a Monastery Garden', 'Bells Across the Meadows', or 'In a Persian Market'. We all sat round the table, silent, spellbound, admiring – all except me. I tried to look bored with these silly sentimental pieces and prayed that some of the notes would stick. They never did. The discoloured keys responded to his touch as if he were playing a Steinway so that one of the neighbours would say next morning, 'Got a new piano, Mrs Storey?'

Eventually the soldiers from the searchlight battery were posted to another part of the country but Trevor had made sufficient impression upon my parents for them to name their youngest child after him when he was born at the end of the war.

There were other novelties and other sorrows during those first two or three years of the war. Our street, which had once known no more than the passing of haycarts and the occasional motor-car, now shuddered with the noise of tanks on summer manoeuvres, their tracks leaving impressions like large zip-fasteners in the road where we still tried to play whip-n-top and fag-cards.

There are no family photographs of these years. Film became scarce, then unobtainable, and the only picture we have in the shoe-box is of Uncle Joe who was lost at Dunkirk in 1940. Uncle Joe was my mother's stepbrother, the only son of her mother's second marriage. I only knew of this uncle from the conversations between my mother and her mother when she came over from Sawtry to visit us, which was either early spring or autumn. It is an autumn visit I remember most. She arrived one morning with a basketful of blackberries and a dead hare, which Uncle Joe had shot.

'There you are, Kit', she said to my mother as she put the hare on the kitchen table. 'That should make a decent dinner for you.'

It was strange to hear my mother called by this first name, which was not the name she was given, anyway. Her name was Sarah but she was always known as Mam, even by my father, and only her sisters-in-law called her by her Christian name. Why grandma from Sawtry called her Kit was never explained. I liked it and wished it was the name by which she could always be known.

I looked at the dead hare with a mixture of wonder and horror.

'Why's it dead?'

'It's bin shot, boy, that's why.'

'Who shot it?'

'Your uncle.'

'Does he always shoot things?'

She laughed and ruffled my hair. 'Good Lord, no. He's one of the gentlest men you could wish to meet.'

'Then why did he shoot the hare?'

'Because it was eating all the vegetables in my garden ... Now you go off and play so that I can have a bit of peace and quiet with your mother.'

I did not go out immediately but stood at the table and stroked the fur of the hare, hoping that it would come back to life. But I was no St Francis and the animal stayed cold and dead. Then I saw the small hole in its neck where the bullet had entered. There was a ring of dried blood and the blood was dark. I let my fingers burrow into the thick, coarse coat and held one of the long, stiff paws in my hand. Those legs had once been free, had leapt over fields and dykes, had known part of the world I have never seen. I put my thumb on its clouded eyes, then lightly outlined its ears. I was quite sure that I would never like Uncle Joe if I ever met him.

Such pious feelings were forgotten a few days later when grandfather skinned the animal and gave me the skin to take over to the rag-and-bone man who lived almost opposite. I had often seen my grandfather skin a rabbit, or ring a chicken's neck, and it never occurred to me that he was cruel, so why Uncle Joe? I ran off to see how much I would get for such a fine skin. No more than three or four pence, I imagine.

I was to meet Joe the hare-killer just two or three weeks before he embarked for France during the first year of the war. His coarse khaki uniform and polished badges made him a popular visitor and I found him as gentle as grandma said he was. To mark this occasion my father suggested we should get Mr Anthony the photographer to come along and take a picture outside our back door. He set up his tripod, selected a glass-plate and then disappeared under a large, black velvet shawl draped over his head and camera. Uncle Joe was not a natural smiler, nor did he really look much of a soldier. He was a taciturn man with no ambitions for becoming a hero. He did not relish the idea of going over to France and wished only to go back to his village and a job on the land. He sat on a kitchen chair, stared at the camera lens and failed to respond to Mr Anthony's plea to 'smile please!' In fifteen minutes it was all over and Joe stayed until teatime. We never saw him again.

A few months later grandma arrived in pouring rain and stood at our door. She was dressed wholly in black and tears were streaming down her face. Mother had a job to persuade her to step into the house and said quietly, 'What's the matter?'

The tears were no longer silent. 'He's gone', she sobbed. 'He's gone, Kit. Joe's gone!'

I looked on, puzzled and only half-understanding. Where had he gone? Slowly the fragments of grandma's narrative began to make sense. Uncle Joe was among the many thousands of soldiers who were evacuated from Dunkirk in 1940 and the boat into which he had climbed was blown up. Those who could not swim, like Joe, were drowned, or shot by the German planes flying low over the survivors.

In her grief, grandma sat there cursing Hitler and God. 'I'll never believe there's a God now, Kit, never!' Her small, ashen face gained no colour as she leaned towards the fire, rocking backwards and forwards, saying 'never, never ...' and clenching her hands until their knuckles grew white as ivory. My mother stayed with her all the time, trying to comfort her. She was similar in build and features but very strong and reassuring. 'We're not alone, Mum. There must be hundreds like us. You can't blame God.' But grandma knew that no comfort, comparison, faith or consolation could ever bring back her son. 'That blessed war was nothing to do with him', she said in an accusing tone. 'He shouldn't have been taken like that.'

I went out into the garden, still wet with rain, and wondered how long such sorrow would last. I kicked idly among the stones on the path at the bottom of the garden where the chicken-run had been. I took out my pocket-knife and whittled away at a piece of wood until it was no more than a matchstick. The day had been stopped in its progress. Finding nothing else to do I walked back to the house, stopping for a moment to look at the blistered paintwork on the kitchen door which had been the backcloth for Uncle Joe's portrait. Inside the house grandma was drinking a cup of tea and my mother was now cooking a meal. On the table was a belated birthday present for me – *The Mystery of Manor Pool*. 'I know you like reading', grandma said in a distant voice.

By late afternoon it was time for her to leave and we walked with her to the bus-stop. I had the feeling that I would never see her again either. But she must have come to see us once more because one day a framed enlargement of the photograph of Uncle Joe appeared above our mantelpiece. There he was, a sad man dressed in Khaki, his regimental badge permanently bull-shone, his forced and fixed smile hiding the fear of war – a young man nailed up on our wall, pretending he was a soldier. As children we grew to accept his grey face. His eyes seemed to follow us round the room for the next twenty years. It was finally taken down when we moved house and it was like living his death again.

As well as the photograph grandma also brought me a pair of blue and white football socks and a pair of shin-guards. 'You can have these now', she said, 'they used to be Joe's.' I put them on and ran out into the street to show off in front of the other children.

'Where'd you git 'em?', they asked.

'They were my uncle's. He used to play for Tottenham Hotspur.'

'Liar!'

'It's true. He's just been killed by the Germans for trying to blow up Hitler's headquarters.'

'Liar again!' they shouted, and began pushing me about. One of the boys who disliked me punched me on the shoulder and said, 'You're a bloody big mouth, Storey.'

'You're only jealous', I replied, and walked away, hoping that my latest acquisitions would persuade the teacher that it was now time for me to make my appearance in the school's football team. It worked, once. I was put on the right wing for the first half of the match, then switched to left back. As most of the action was taking place at the other end of the field I found myself daydreaming so that when there was an attack from the opposition I was rather taken by surprise. As their Centre-forward raced towards our goal with the ball at his feet the teacher shouted, 'Stop him, Storey! Stop him!' But the distance between us was too great, *and* the skill no doubt. We lost one nil and I was never given another chance to prove that if only I could have played in the right position I might have been another Tom Finny.

I was still taken down to the field whenever we had sport

but was demoted to linesman or ball-boy or just left to roam about looking into the hedgerows or keeping company with the cows at the far end of the field. I can remember them more than the other boys but for a different reason perhaps.

1940–45

9 Blind love in the wings

Having made more progress with my cornet-playing than I
did with the piano or any other lessons, my father decided to
buy me a new instrument for my next birthday. It was a
frosted silver-plated Besson with mother-of-pearl valve-caps
and a lyre for holding the music should I ever have to play on
the march. New instruments were already difficult to acquire
in these early years of the war so I knew that he had gone to a
lot of trouble to get one for me.

I thought I was getting a new pair of pyjamas for my
birthday, so when I went downstairs for breakfast I was
puzzled to see a black leather case on the table.

'Well, you'd better see what's inside it', said father, unable
to contain his own excitement any longer.

When I opened the lid and saw the cornet dazzling with a
brightness that made it almost untouchable, I gasped. 'Is it
really mine?'

After a few moments of gloating over it and tentatively
laying my fingers on the shining silver, I was asked to play
something. I might just as well have been asked to fly. I put
the cornet to my lips but they were dry and a lump came into
my throat. The first sound I made was brief and crude. Surely
an instrument like this should play itself, I thought.

'Give it time to warm up', said father. 'A new instrument
needs playing in. It's bound to feel strange for a while.'

I tried again and this time a melody slowly emerged which
had a brighter tone than I had ever managed before. I gained
confidence and played the whole piece. My mother stood
looking on with pride and said, 'I hope you realize what a
lucky boy you are.'

As well as my cornet-playing I now had to study the theory
of music and, once a week, went on the local bus to the

neighbouring village of Farcet to have lessons from a man who had once been a Salvation Army bandmaster and had passed several examinations. Soon the intricacies of major and minor keys, of augmented fifths and diminished sevenths, of time-signatures and transposition began to interest me as much as playing, so much so that my ambitions turned more towards being a composer than a performer. Instead of books of adventure stories I now read *Harmony and Composition* by Stewart Macpherson and changed my weekly comic *Hotspur* to the *British Bandsman*. I may not have been able to work out simple mathematical problems at school but I was capable of analysing sonata-form and beginning to understand something about fugue, exposition and recapitulation. Each week I looked through the *Radio Times* to see when there was a programme of brass band music. I then conducted this in front of the oval mirror above our mantelpiece so that I could watch myself going through a display of extravagant gestures as each piece was performed. I made myself a long baton from a willow tree, painting it white and giving it a cork handle. For the rest of that year I guided every top-class band in the country through some of their most outstanding broadcasts. I do not think I have ever had more enthusiasm for anything in my life than music. But enthusiasm is not enough. If there was any talent there it fell far short of my expectations and, in the end, I had to settle for the local parish hall rather than the Royal Albert Hall, just as some boys have to settle for the village green rather than Wembley or Lords. Mine was not an isolated failure, only a bitter disappointment. But I did not know then that I would have to give up music and turn instead to writing. That came much later.

In the year that I received my new cornet I also received my first invitation to play in public. A group of young people under the direction of Mrs Ivy Turner, had created a show called *Youth has its Fling*, for the purpose of raising money for charity and, probably, the war effort. Bill Heard, who was not only the talent scout but also master of ceremonies and star singer, called at our house one Sunday morning to ask if I would like to join the company as a guest and play a couple of solos in their next production. The answer, of course, did not rest with me and my father was very apprehensive about it to begin with. He wanted to know more about the show. Who was in it, who was in charge and how late would it finish? Mr Heard patiently answered all these questions and assured my father that all the people connected with the show came from good families and that I would come to no harm. 'We have our own band with Brian Turner, Peter Mackrell and Ronnie Martell. There's a comedy duo with Charlie Pateman and Alan Searle; a female vocalist, a conjuror and ventriloquist; then there's Gwelma Hay with her troupe of dancers – Barbara Bingham, Hilda Reynolds, Iris Rust, Eileen Burdett – it's all good clean fun and we like to encourage local talent.'

Father pondered on this for another moment or two, then looked at me. 'Would you like to play in this gentleman's concert?' I nodded, wondering at the same time what father would choose for me to play.

Bill Heard was obviously delighted with our decision and said, 'If this show is a success there will be others and we would like to think your son could become a regular attraction. If you could let me have the titles of his solos as soon as you can I'll make sure we get them printed in the programme.' Then he shook hands with us and left.

Although there was a glimmer of pride in father's face I think he was equally concerned about my mixing with so many Tories. 'You needn't start getting ideas above your station', he said. 'They'll only want you for as long as they need you.' He often recalled a Member of Parliament for the Isle of Ely who stood on Whittlesey's market-place during one election campaign and said, 'The working-class are like potatoes; they should be buried in the winter and dug up when needed.' He was suspicious of any offer of help or friendship from people who belonged to any political party other than his own. But, his prejudice did not stand in my way and, by the end of the morning, it was agreed that the three pieces I should prepare were 'Love's Old Sweet Song', 'Trees', and 'There'll Be Bluebirds Over the White Cliffs of Dover'. It was also made abundantly clear to me that from now on I would need to put in much more practice.

By the time the night of the performance arrived I felt I could have played my solos on anything from a watering-can to a church organ. I heard them in my sleep, at school, and while I ate my meals. My cornet had been polished even beyond its nascent brightness. It now threw off diamonds. My shoes were similarly bright, my hair Brylcreemed, my white shirt starched until its collar was as sharp as a guillotine. As I walked through the streets with my mother I felt as proud as someone making his debut in London. The British Legion hall to which I was going was used more often for whist-drives and auction sales and had nothing like the atmosphere of a theatre. But that didn't matter.

Before the show began I was taken on stage by Bill Heard and shown where I had to stand. The stage felt empty and unreal with the curtains closed. I smelt the freshly painted scenery and looked round at the bower of artificial roses, the cardboard veranda, the open door through which no one could walk, and the windows that could not be broken. One of the spotlights came on in the wings and, for a moment, I winced under its fierce glare. On the other side of the curtains I could hear the audience settling into its seats. Somewhere among that waiting crowd sat my mother, trembling for me. My father was either working or perhaps too scared to sit through my performance.

'Are you frightened?' Bill asked.

'A little bit.'

'That's good. It pays to feel a bit nervous before you go on. We all do, so don't worry. Just try to relax.'

I think I was more excited than nervous. After my insular existence this was a new experience for me to be among people who laughed, joked, teased each other and generally had a good time together. I took to Bill and the rest of the company immediately. Because I was the youngest – and a bit of a curiosity – they made a fuss of me, which I didn't mind at all. Bill was a smart young man with auburn hair and a good voice. He included in his repertoire several popular songs of the day, but the favourites with his fans were Jerome Kern's 'All the Things You Are' and 'Long Ago and Far Away'. The words and melodies have remained with me ever since and I often find myself singing them in unguarded moments of nostalgia.

Back in the makeshift dressing-rooms I caught something of the first-night excitement among the rest of the cast. Many of them had been through it before but teased each other and made jokes about fluffed lines during rehearsals. Not one of them was as green as their new guest artist, however, and when the call for 'Beginners Please!' went round I thought it meant me, so I made my way on to the stage. Fortunately, one of the young dancers saw my error and grabbed me back just in time before the band struck-up with the show's signature-tune – 'Whispering' – and a flurry of dancing-girls swept on from the wings for their first number. I wiped the sweat from my brow as I realized how silly I would have looked in the middle of all those painted legs and fish-net stockings. Bill calmed me down and said he would tell me when it was my turn. When that moment came I was just as eager to begin. I walked on stage and became aware of the expectant silence that had suddenly descended on the audience. I was so astonished by the sound of my first few notes as they rang out that I nearly forgot which piece I should be playing first. Then I remembered my grandfather's advice – 'play the words and you'll be all right.' I no longer seemed in charge of what I was doing. I was taken over by some great feeling welling up within me and played without making any mistakes and, I'm sure, in a way that I had never played before. As the last notes of that first item died away I heard the audience burst into applause and shout for more. I looked over the footlights to see if my mother was clapping too, but it was dark in the hall and all I could see were rows of shadows and a haze of cigarette smoke.

For my next number I played 'Love's Old Sweet Song' and experienced a new thrill as the audience joined in the chorus – 'Just a song at twilight …' Because I had not expected this I enjoyed the sensation even more, appreciating even at that age that there is something special happening when performer and audience become one. It was, I suppose, an awareness of power, of persuasion and leadership. The seeds of megalomania are sown very early. Even louder applause greeted the end of this piece and I was asked to play an encore. When I finally walked off stage the girl who had first saved me from going on too soon, bent down and kissed me. This surpassed all the approval I had received from the audience and I fell in love with her immediately. What I did not know then was that she was already in love with someone else of her own age and I hadn't a chance.

In the broken-down museum of a shoe-box I also found a local press-cutting from those days which reported that 'Master E. Storey contributed several cornet solos most effectively.' So it *was* true! I had not been deceived by memory or vanity. Well, certainly not by memory.

I appeared in *Youth has its Fling* quite a few times after that and loved the work behind the scenes as much as the performances. I was amused to see how a false beard or a stick of make-up could change the familiar face of a solicitor's clerk or a nurseryman's son into a feeble octogenarian, washerwoman or clown. I began to think that it would not be a bad idea to become an actor, anything to be part of that world of illusion, to be something other than what one was, to be a voice behind a mask.

Sometimes the show was invited to play for one-night stands in the neighbouring villages of Coates, Eye and Thorney. Travelling home late at nights on those lonely fenland roads during war-time blackouts was often a show in itself. The poor driver, with very restricted headlights (which were no more than slits over the main lamps) occasionally took the wrong turning or got lost altogether, especially if it was foggy. We did not mind how lost the driver was for there was always a lot of fun to be had after our performance and we no longer had to worry about an audience. We were the audience as well as the performers. As the old bus lurched and swaggered between dykes and hedges, jokes were retold, sketches rewritten, and rowdy songs improvised. These were usually based on well-known tunes which ranged from 'Knees Up, Mother Brown' to 'Onward Christian Soldiers'. But the most popular was 'Roll me over in the clover, roll me over lay me down and do it again, which went on for ten verses, each verse getting more ribald as the miles went by. Then, slowly the voices tired and the couples on the back seat became more engrossed in quieter pursuits. Thus, loaded with its band of strolling players, the snub-nosed, cocoa-coloured bus crawled like a hedgehog back to town. To a more sophisticated mind it would not be as romantic now but it was a lively experience then for a ten-year-old boy who had been rather cosseted.

Sadly the war was to take some of the most able young men into the Armed Services and they could not be replaced.

The drummer, the pianist, the stage-manager and master of ceremonies, all had to leave the company, some went into the Army, at least one into the Navy, and when the news reached us that first one, then another, had been killed in action we were shocked into stony disbelief. Their deaths robbed the show of its youthfulness and vitality and, before the war ended, the company was disbanded and the surviving talent went elsewhere.

One of my next appearances was at the Newell's Engineering Works in Fletton, where my father now worked as a jig-borer. Most factories then went in for some kind of lunch-time entertainment, the sort of thing made popular by such BBC programmes as *Workers' Playtime* and *Music While You Work*, and based on the same morale-boosting idea of ENSA (which quickly earned the nickname *Every Night Something Awful*.)

My father came home one day and said he had been asked by the leader of a well-known dance band if I would play at one of their lunch-time concerts, so a date was arranged and, on the morning of my engagement I left the house with my suit well-pressed and my hair plastered down with cream. Mother walked to the end of the street with me, carrying my music-stand, and waited at The Packhorse Inn bus-stop until the bus arrived. But, just before it did, a bird flew overhead and dropped a large yellow splodge down my face and on to the lapel of my jacket. I was mortified and wanted to go back home. 'Don't be ridiculous', said my mother. 'It's a sign of good luck. Give me your hankie ...' She cleaned me as best she could and saw me on to the bus. 'You'd better play well this time', she said, 'your father will hear you today.'

I was met at the factory gates and taken into the canteen where all the workers had gathered for their lunch. It was very noisy and stuffy. The band sounded extremely loud and, for the first time, I felt frightened rather than nervous or excited. I did not play well, despite the good-luck omen from the bird. Afterwards the band-leader said to me, 'You get the notes right, son, but you need to loosen up a bit, y'know, take a few risks. You're playing too straight at the moment for this kind of music. You wanna make them bluebirds really fly, like this ...' And he did an impersonation of Louis Armstrong, screeching some high notes into the smoky atmosphere that did not appeal to me at all. I preferred to play straight and it was a long time before I learned to appreciate real jazz.

It was whilst my father worked at this factory that he had his hand smashed in one of the jig-borers and had to be rushed to hospital. The news caused great distress at home and mother asked Mrs Redhead, our next-door neighbour, to look after us while she went through to Peterborough Hospital to find out how badly hurt father was. It was, if I remember correctly, a Sunday. Although my father's hand had been severely crushed the surgeon had been able to perform an emergency operation and save it from further mutilation. It meant that father was in hospital for several weeks and then at home for many months. When the plaster had been removed Nurse Berry came each day to dress his wound and we became very fond of her. She was a jovial, breezy character and her cheerful manner helped to lift the frequent depression that affected us all. She arrived with her black bag and turned the front room into a hospital ward with an array of bowls, bandages, cotton-wool, ointments and disinfectant which left a surgical smell in the house for the next couple of days.

Then began the long legal battle with the firm over compensation, which ended with my father being awarded several hundred pounds. His hand never functioned properly after that accident and, having lost his job, he had to find work elsewhere. At the same time he was fined for riding his bicycle without a rear-light and, although the lamp was proved to be faulty, he had to pay up. 'I shan't be sorry when this year's over', he got into the habit of saying. 'That must have been a bad coin I put out last New Year's Eve.' He was, at times, a superstitious man and always hid some money outside the house on 31 December and brought it in on 1 January. With it came your luck. He was to have another spell in hospital before his final illness and that was when he had a hip-replacement. By this time he was more passive and less certain about fate controlling our lives. I remember driving home after one of my visits to him and seeing the fens almost like a hospital ward, grey and depressed under a weeping sky –

This is where on skimping days
the crippled sky leans on crutches

of telegraph-poles, aching under the weight
of what should have been cloud.

You can see its cramped hand
pulling along wires that crackle
between distances, bowed like a husband
returning home at the wrong time.

Is it too lame to hear, or does
it go limping to eavesdrop on those
taking advantage of the day to speak
of things they might not say

if earth spoke openly with the sun?
Why, when darkness hums with gossip,
let daylight in to cut the line
we were not meant to ring?

Do we not all at some time feel that our affairs are beyond
our control, that we have accidentally been caught up in a
conversation that is really no concern of ours, that we are
going in a direction we did not choose to go, like getting on to
the wrong train by mistake?

Certainly the direction that my next few years were to take
were not so much an act of fate as an accident of
circumstance. My education at the junior mixed school was
coming to an end and I, with all the other children of my age,
had to sit an entrance examination at the grammar school in
March, to see if we were good enough to continue our
schooling there. If not it meant that we, the boys, would be
sent to the Church of England Senior Boys School in Station
Road, a place with a reputation for strict discipline and
corporal punishment. We all knew at the age of eleven that if
we wished to avoid spending the rest of our school life at that
institution we had to do well at the examination. March was
a small fenland town nineteen miles away and as unknown to
most of us as Tahiti. It would be an achievement even if we
got there on the day.

I can see now that the examination was the farce of a
lifetime but its outcome then could not have been more
important – or more casual. Somewhere between those
periods of daytime sleeping at our desks and playing

war-games in air-raid shelters, we must have been told about the examination but I do not remember any preparation for it at all. As places were scarce and very few children needed to pass, the majority of us were left to flounder.

Our last year at Broad Street was just like any other, with one exception. Mr Lambert, who was our teacher, was killed one morning while cycling to school and the news left us saddened and bewildered. He had always been strict with us and could hit an ear with a piece of chalk wherever you sat in the room. His ruler also kept a few knuckles tingling when he was displeased with our behaviour, but we had respect for him and his death was particularly tragic at a time when there were few men teachers left in the schools.

As far as I can remember the first that we knew about sitting the entrance examination was when we received instructions one morning to report to the local railway station the following Saturday where a train would take us to March. There we would be met and taken to the school where we would be given question-papers which we had to complete with the correct answers in a given time and, 'If you are intelligent enough to pass – and if your parents can afford it – you will become a grammar school pupil. If you don't, you will all go down to that establishment in Station Road, and you know what that means.'

Did I realize what a momentous journey it was when the train pulled out of Whittlesey station that morning and we hurtled over a landscape that had so far only meant pleasure, holidays, freedom? I doubt it, for in my heart of hearts I knew it was a wasted trip.

At the school we were sorted out into groups and led into a large classroom where, in one morning, we were to be judged – not for what we had done, or not done up to the age of eleven, but for what we were going to do, or not do, for the rest of our lives. Now *we* felt like refugees, lost and bemused, stared at and picked over to see if we were acceptable for that better world. But did we know then that the verdict would make all the difference between a good job and a dull job, or that failure would mean that we would be expected to work for several pounds a month less than someone in the same office who had been lucky enough to go to grammar school? If we had been told it had gone in one ear and out the other.

As far as I can recall, only two or three boys out of our class of forty passed and they, we had to admit, were naturally bright anyway and came from homes where they would have been encouraged to work to that end. Some of the other clever ones, who did not get into March Grammer School, were sent by their parents to schools in Peterborough. As my parents could not afford then to pay for my education I think they were sadly relieved that I had failed to win a place and would do well enough down at Station Road.

I can still remember the gloom of that examination room with its rows of desks, the pens that wouldn't write, and the green question-papers that might have been written in a foreign language for all that I knew. My nib was crossed, the ink smudged, and the eyes of the invigilator looked down on me with a sadistic sneer. I was overcome by despair and looked longingly out of the window at the sky, praying for an escape.

After the examination most of us shambled dejectedly into the fresh air, knowing that our futures were sealed. We sought the nearest sweet-shop for consolation and bought some lemonade. The shopkeeper was a fat, jolly woman who cheered us up by getting us to say in chorus 'Wee-wee!' as she served our drinks. Hearing of our morning's tribulations she said, 'Oh, I shouldn't worry about them silly old exams. I've never taken an exam in my life and look at me, I've managed to 'ave eight children.' What that had to do with our academic prospects was beyond me.

We made our way back to the station to take the return journey to Whittlesey. The fens, which always look spacious, looked overwhelmingly vast that day, making our fears, our very existence, appear almost insignificant. What were we but little things crawling back home to whatever it was fate – or circumstance – had kept for us! If I had to get a job out in those fields what harm would that do me? I would be doing no less than what my family had done for generations. If the land meant that much to me what shame was there in working on it?

'If we're lucky enough', said Ernie Brown. 'This war will last long enough for us to be called up and then we shan't have to worry about a job.'

I waited patiently to hear the results. They were as feared.

In September 1941 I became an inmate of the Senior Boys School in Station Road and came face to face with the headmaster – Mr Bertram Walker.

10   Miss Speechley framed in snow

On that first morning we stood in front of the rest of the school and heard our headmaster say in his calculating way, 'Look at them! These are the new boys who have arrived to commence their education. You were like that once. I hope you will set them an excellent example of what we all expect here.'

Mr Walker was a headmaster of the nineteenth century and believed his cane to be as important an implement as a set square. He had a way of making you feel grateful and ill at ease at the same time. With a few well-chosen words he convinced us all of our guilt, naïvety, privilege or deprivation. He was always immaculately dressed in a tweed suit, complete with watch-chain hanging from his waistcoat pocket, and a voluminous handkerchief in his breast pocket. He insisted on good deportment and said to us that morning, 'Stand up straight. You are not apes now. You are human beings – at least in the making. Pull your shoulders back.'

After this baptism we were introduced to Miss Clark, who was to be our teacher for the first year. Miss Ethel Clark had taught our fathers and we knew of her reputation for being fierce, strict and unforgiving. 'You'd better be careful', my father warned. 'She's got eyes in the back of her head.' She handed out some hymn-books and told us to stand by the desks which had been allotted to us – two boys to a desk, two classes to a room. The headmaster then sat down at the piano, played the opening bars of the first hymn – 'Fight the Good Fight', and we began to sing.

The Order of Service could have been in Japanese. The prayers, the Apostles Creed, the Responses, were all strange to our ears and we obviously demonstrated to the rest of the assembly that not only were we illiterate but also pagan. For most of us this was our first contact with the Church of England's way of worship.

Afterwards Miss Clark peered accusingly at us through her steel-rimmed spectacles and said, 'It is clear to me that the first thing I shall have to teach you is the Creed. So, you will now say after me, 'I believe in God ... the Father Almighty ... Maker of Heaven and Earth ...' Solemnly and parrot-like we repeated each phrase until we came to the end, then we started all over again. Slowly, like another multiplication table, the meaningless words began to sink in, to form a pattern and rhythm in our heads that made them stick until we were word-perfect if not wholly converted. They were words we were never allowed to forget. Quite unexpectedly, in the middle of another lesson, Miss Clark would snap at a boy who was not paying attention ... 'Right, Brown! What is the next line after "Was crucified, dead and buried?" Come on!' Brown hesitated for a few seconds, rose from his seat (for we were never allowed to remain seated when answering a question) and said in an uncertain voice – "He descended into hell", Miss.' We thought from the tone of his voice and the expression on his face that he was about to suggest that Miss Clark followed the same route, but he refrained.

In addition to our daily worship, the morning assembly was also the time at which yesterday's offenders were punished and, as the school seemed to have more rebels than angels, the cane was a regular feature of these gatherings. The roll-call was predictable – Knight ... Garner ... Oliver ... Smith ...' Familiar names, familiar hands outstretched. Hands that seldom flinched under the swish of sudden pain. Hands that afterwards clenched in their desire to hit back. When, we wondered, would our time come? What crime would we have to commit to warrant such fierce correction? The crimes varied but the punishment was the same, varying only in the number of strokes given to each hand or leg. The offenders could have been found guilty of rough behaviour in the playground, smoking in the outdoor lavatories, disobedience, arrogance, truancy, stealing, breaking rank as we filed into school, or just consistently bad class-work. The regular culprits claimed they had devised ways of lessening the sting of the cane by fixing strands of horsehair to their palms, or rubbing their skins with a raw onion. To have a hand that could resist a cane until it broke made a boy a school hero. There were few of these and only once did I see a boy retaliate. He was a big lad, used to punishment, but one morning he decided that he'd had enough. He grabbed the cane from the headmaster and started lashing out at him. We didn't particularly like the boy, who was a bully, but we were impressed by his courage, or impulsive action, which meant that the Head had to be rescued by three of his female staff. In fact, all the teachers at the school were women and they had a tough time trying to maintain order among so many fen-tigers.

Smoking was the one crime for which most boys were punished at some time in their first year at the senior school, which was ironic as the headmaster was himself a heavy smoker and sometimes asked his prefects to go to the shops to get him some more cigarettes. We could not afford packets of fags so collected 'dog-ends' and rolled our own, or shared out those stolen from our fathers' supply. 'You can even make fags out of tea-leaves', said Ernie Brown one day when we had run out of second-hand tobacco.

'You do know that smoking will stunt your growth', said Alan one morning in the lavatory. 'You could end up a dwarf.'

'It's like masturbating', said Ken. 'You'll go blind if you do it more than twice a day.'

But school was not all hymn-singing and corporal punishment. The Head had a difficult task to perform during those war years when classes were overcrowded and teachers scarce. He had the assistance of four – Miss Clark, Mrs Colbert, Miss Speechley and Mrs Walker, his wife. The first and third year classes were held in the same room where we all gathered each morning for assembly, so it was not surprising that we sometimes got our subjects confused. When I was in Miss Clark's class I found it more interesting to listen to what was going on in Mrs Colbert's third form at the other end of the room. There were two smaller classrooms, for the second and fourth years, one divided from the main hall by a wooden partition, the other by a brick wall. Above them was a splendid ceiling of timbered arches to which we frequently projected arrows made out of broken pen-nibs. When I revisited the school recently to see how the building had been converted into a Roman Catholic Church I was surprised to discover how small it all was.

Each of the classrooms had either an open fire or an old tortoise-stove in the corner which provided us with heat in winter. On each of the stoves stood a bucket of water slowly emitting steam into the stuffy air. It was the class-prefect's job to keep the fire well-fed and the bucket full. Sometimes the water boiled so furiously that clouds of vapour filled the room and it felt as if our classes were being conducted in a laundry. But we grew attached to those old stoves. They were part of our class and we half-expected them one morning to answer to a name on the register – 'Brown ... Curtis ... Greenwood ... Storey ... Stove ...'

The main hall was also used for communal singing-lessons. The headmaster was fond of music, especially singing. He sat at the piano and, from a position where he could see us all, did his best to coax good diction and a tuneful sound from our flat, wide-vowelled, fenland voices. They were usually rousing songs, such as 'Who Were the Yeomen, the Yeomen of England?', good, solid patriotic affirmations of Britain's greatness when we were constantly threatened with invasion by Adolf Hitler.

It was only in these singing-lessons that Mr Walker was able to make us laugh by pulling faces and imitating our strained style. 'You open your mouths as if you are all Cheshire cats. Learn to open your mouths wide and round, like this ...' He pursed his lips and then stretched them into a large O as he pulled in his cheeks. 'And sing from your chest, not your throat ... You must breathe from the diaphragm ...' He put his hand on his stomach and took a deep breath. 'Come on, let me see you do it. Put your hands there, like that and breathe in ... Can you feel it? Fill your lungs. Now, breathe slowly out ... very slowly. And again ...' But, by this time we were giggling too much to control anything and we turned to our next song which was all about Nelson, or Drake, or someone else who had made England great.

My first year in Miss Clark's class came to an end and after the summer holidays, I went up to class two where the teacher was Miss Speechley. She had a gift for understanding the boys who came into her care. She exercised discipline with kindness, authority with dignity, instruction with enthusiasm. She seldom sent a boy to be caned and if she did it was always with regret. I owe her a special debt because it was through her that I first became aware of the joys of English literature. It was a modest beginning but one which I now recognize with belated gratitude.

We must have had English lessons on other days of the week but it is the Friday afternoon period at the end of the day which claims my affection. We sat, our arms folded on our desks, and watched Miss Speechley as she mounted her lectern-desk and began to read the next episode of *Oliver Twist, A Tale of Two Cities, Tom Sawyer, Vice Versa* or *Treasure Island.* As television had not arrived in our homes to take over our imaginations, forty very different Fagins or Long John Silvers haunted the alleys of our minds as our teacher led us through each chapter. *Black Beauty* and *Lorna Doone* were also part of our Friday afternoon fare and it was a marvellous way to end the school week. Miss Speechley had a knack of ending on a dramatic climax which she knew would guarantee our attendance in school the following Friday. Very few boys played truant in her class.

Because of the influx of evacuees, not only were our classrooms overcrowded but some of the classes had to be accommodated in other buildings in the town – chapel schoolrooms, the parish hall and the British Legion hall were used for that purpose. They were poorly equipped and inadequately heated, grey substitutes for what should have been bright, twentieth-century classrooms with plenty of books and light. The school itself, built in 1851, was cosy by comparison with some of the rooms that were hired. We became a nomadic tribe of learners as we were moved from one building to another.

The classroom where I was to spend some very happy hours was the one tucked away behind the Methodist chapel in our street and, of all the days I enjoyed there, it is again a Friday afternoon that I recall most clearly. The first period was music, in which we sang sea-shanties or rounds. Then, after break, we gathered around Miss Speechley to hear the next instalment of whichever book it was she was reading to us then. As soon as she took her place at her desk we were silent, our minds eager for the next piece of action. She read with a soft, warm voice, full of expression and a love of the spoken word. We sat spellbound and I, for one, seldom wanted the afternoon to end. There was one occasion when she was reading of someone like Little Nell trudging through the snow that I felt sure I was there. My own hands became blue with cold. My eyes hurt with the whiteness swirling before them. I looked up at the windows. Large white flakes were floating down in timeless spirals of silence. They lodged on the window-sill and quietly filled up the yard. Did Charles Dickens have such power to make fiction appear reality? Was I dreaming, or was this actually happening? I felt a familiar shudder of excitement when faced with such a possibility, as if I had stepped into the pages of the book and was now part of the story. Miss Speechley continued reading and the snow kept falling. Then, at a quarter-to-four, she reverently closed the book and placed it in the drawer of her desk, which she finally locked. We pleaded for another page, just a hint of what was to come. But it was no good. She only smiled and said, 'You will find out next week ... Stand for prayers.' The drama, tragedy, suspense, pathos, were all over for another seven days and we were dismissed. It was only when I ran out into the school yard that I discovered the snow was real. It not only filled the yard but also our street and the town. We stepped into winter as if we had been awoken from another season, a different time, a make-believe world. The railings where we had so recently played fag-cards were white and I knew that if I walked to the end of our street I would see five thousand acres of whiteness with the fens under snow – but no Little Nell. The spell had been broken.

There were times on those Friday afternoons, when I stayed behind to clean out the fire-grate or help Miss Speechley put her books away, that I would take advantage of the moment and ask her to read the next episode to me. She would never allow me to know ahead of the rest of the class but frequently read something from a different book so that I should not be disappointed. She explained how books came to be written, how authors loved using words, how the imagination created scenes in the mind and what skills were required to put those scenes on paper. 'You must learn not only how to spell but how to construct a sentence in the right way ... that is why you must pay more attention to your grammar, young man.' It was never one of my strengths and, apart from these casual references, I do not think much time was spent on the mechanics of the English language. It took us all our time to remember what nouns, adjectives and verbs were. What Miss Speechley did do, however, was to instil into me a need to read as much as I could, by mentioning authors such as Sir Walter Scott, H.G.Wells and R.M.Ballantyne as well as Dickens. I know now that those extra minutes she spent with me on Friday afternoons went a long way towards the first stirrings of my own ambitions to be a writer. The seeds were planted then even though many years were to pass before I was aware of them. Sadly, Miss Speechley died before a word of mine appeared in print, so she never had the satisfaction of knowing that the unpaid overtime invested in me bore some fruit. She, with Dr Bernard, must share a large part in whatever love for language and literature was eventually to possess me.

Remembering her quiet ways, her greying hair combed tightly back into a bun, and her reserved smile, I am still impressed by the influence she had over that large class of boys, many of whom would have rather been anywhere than in school. Each day she was met at the end of the street and escorted to the schoolroom. We argued amongst ourselves for the privilege of wheeling her old-fashioned bicycle, or of carrying her books. It was the same going home. I can see now that she was probably longing to get on to the seat and pedal home as fast as she could to be rid of us for a few hours, but her care and concern for us during the day were never in question.

Waking up as late as I did to the advantages of some education, I began to show much more interest in other subjects as well. I was attracted to geography more than history, and to music more than English, but I'd had my curiosity whetted and, unlike those days in the infants' school when I never put up my hand to ask a question, now I couldn't keep it down. My third year at the school was spent in Mrs Colbert's class and I was both delighted and surprised when I was awarded the year's prize. I received a copy of Mark Twain's *Huckleberry Finn*, in which had been inscribed – *To EDWARD STOREY, FOR EVENTUALLY REACHING THE TOP. – DECEMBER, 1942.*

I began dipping into its pages as I walked home, letting my

eyes light on any phrase which took my fancy – 'The sun was up so high when I waked that I judged it was after eight o'clock. I laid there in the grass and cool shade, thinking about things ...'

I did not lie in the grass but sat on a tombstone in St Mary's churchyard, reading until the clock chimed five. Although some of the dialect baffled me I cherished the prize then and still have it on my bookshelves.

The following year I graduated to my fourth and final class at the C. of E. Senior Boys School, Station Road, where I was made head prefect with another boy, Ernie Greenwood. This was a position which meant, among other tasks, staying behind after school on Friday afternoons to help get out the County Library books for the people who came in the evening. The school was, at that time, the town's only public lending library and, for just two hours a week, the natives of Whittlesey had the chance to change, or renew, their reading for the following week. This duty gave me my first real contact with any quantity and choice of books and I was amazed at the variety available, even in that limited stock of well-worn volumes. I spent a good deal of the time browsing through each section – *Poetry and Drama, Biographies, Novels* and *Adventure*, much to the annoyance of my fellow prefect.

'Come on, Storey, we haven't got all day. I want to go fishing. What are you staring at now?'

I held the book up for him to see. 'I wish I could borrow this one, it's a play.'

'Well you can't, so put it back and stack those empty boxes in the corridor.'

I pretended to put the book back on the shelf, then, when Ernie wasn't looking, I hid it in my desk. After we had finished setting out the library books we had to go to the head's house to see if he wanted any errands running. His house at that time adjoined the school and he took full advantage of having plenty of boys around to weed his gardens or fetch his cigarettes. (He later moved to a house called 'Bostonia' in Whitmore Street, but the boys were still called upon to work there in their spare time.)

When we had finished our errands for that day we went round to the cycle shed to collect our bikes and I made an excuse for going back to the classroom to get something I said I had forgotten. 'Don't wait', I told Ernie. 'I'll catch you up.'

Fortunately the door was still unlocked and there was no one about. I opened the desk and took out the copy of *Major Barbara* which I had hidden. I tucked it under my pullover and, feeling as guilty as someone who had just robbed a bank, I ran from the room.

That was the beginning of several illegal borrowings and plays were to become my immediate choice for the next few years. I followed *Major Barbara* with most of Shaw's other plays, of which I thought *Saint Joan* the best, with *The Doctor's Dilemma*, a close second. After these I turned to the novels and, purely by accident, I chose Somerset Maugham's *The Razor's Edge* and *Of Human Bondage*. He was succeeded by an assortment of writers, from Marie Corelli to Aldous Huxley and D.H.Lawrence. One week I even had the nerve to take out a book by Bertrand Russell, which had not been borrowed for five years. Considering my interest in music I was rather slow to borrow books from the music section but, when I did, most of them were from the 'Master Musicians' series, which was to maintain a high standard of biography for the next fifty years or more. I began with a volume on Beethoven, followed by Tchaikovsky and Chopin. Although all these books were borrowed illicitly I felt justified in taking them to make up for my lack of education and always returned them to the right place on the shelf when my pleasure was satisfied.

I was fortunate to have in my last class another sympathetic teacher who encouraged me to pursue my lessons with the same zeal I had gained from Miss Speechley and Mrs Colbert. My new teacher was Mrs Walker (wife of the headmaster) and I think she believed in me more than anyone. 'Although I wouldn't like to lose you, you really ought to be at a grammar school', she said. 'Why ever didn't you pass?' There was no answer to the question then.

To begin with we were, I think, a little in awe of her because she was married to the headmaster, but we need not have worried. She was a kind, dedicated teacher in her own right who seldom lost her temper and I enjoyed being in her class. She, too, took an interest in my music and allowed me to conduct the class choir (which was everyone) or write out tunes on the blackboard. Some of the boys thought I was a creep or a show-off but this did not bother me. From being a child who preferred to stay out of things I was now this awful extrovert.

Most of the boys at that age wanted to leave school as quickly as possible to become wage-earners. I wanted to stay at school for the next ten years and dreaded the thought of having to get a job. My parents noticed how keen I was and, among our weekly papers, we now took the *Children's Newspaper* and I was allowed to listen to plays on the radio.

It was through radio drama that I was introduced to the first piece of contemporary classical music that I was to enjoy for many years – Ravel's Introduction and Allegro for Harp, Flute, Clarinet and Strings, which was the incidental music for the play *The Man Born to be King* by Dorothy L. Sayers. This serial, commissioned by the BBC was very controversial at the time and thousands of listeners were appalled that Christ should be portrayed by an actor and that some of his disciples should speak like the ordinary fishermen that they were. I was not concerned about the arguments (which now seem quite unreasonable) but I eagerly awaited each episode of the play just to hear again Ravel's lovely music.

It could have been the music to accompany my other pastime then – kite-flying. I went with a boy from school and, while we flew our kites, we argued about which bird sang best. I was all for skylarks but Alan thought their song was too shrill and monotonous. He preferred the thrush or robin. But, I said, it's all too easy for them. All they have to do is sit on a fence or a branch and open their beaks. The lark has to take the trouble to rise from the ground and sing into the wind on an invisible perch. 'Besides', I claimed, 'the lark is essentially a fenland bird', which it wasn't, 'and I can't imagine what it would be like not to hear *that* song out here.'

I did not know then that twenty or thirty years ago larks used to be snared in their thousands and sent to London markets. Nor did I know that the field where we flew our kites was the field where my mother's father had been killed in a farming accident sixty years earlier.

The pendulum sun pauses. There is a moment between

seasons, a moment between ages when everything changes. We sat having tea one Sunday afternoon and my father said to me, 'What do you want to do when you leave school?'

I remained silent. I did not want to leave school and had avoided making plans for when I did. Among other things that education did not offer in those days was 'Careers Advice'.

For some reason (which might have been his own lack of confidence) my father always appeared to address my mother when he spoke to anyone else, but I knew who he was really addressing when he said, 'It's time you made up your mind. I'd done two years work by the time I was your age and had no choice in the matter either.'

My sister had already been at work four years and it was clear to me that my own childhood was expected to come to an end before the summer was out.

'So what would you like to do?' my father asked again.

I was more certain of what I did *not* want to do, which was to work in the brickyards or on the land, and the offer I had received to work in a men's outfitters was something I kept to myself. A local accountant, who took an interest in me because of my cornet-playing, also said that I was to go and see him when I left school should I ever want a job. As arithmetic was my worst subject the thought of working all day with figures filled me with dismay and I did not remind my father of that invitation. So, on the spur of the moment I blurted out, 'I'd like to be a reporter on a newspaper.'

It was my father's turn to be silent. This surprised him even more than it did me. Again, he looked at mother. 'Well, I don't know what to say about that, do you? A reporter? What sort of qualifications do you have to have for that? You'd need to know how to do shorthand for one thing, and typing.'

'I would need to know how to do both whatever kind of office I worked in.'

'So you want to work in an office?

'I think so.'

'Well I don't know about that.' Again he looked at mother and smiled. 'He'd be the first white-collar worker we've had in the family.' He rose from his chair as if to bring the discussion to an end. 'I'll think about it … You can go out now, if you want to.'

I went out for a bike ride and looked over the fens with a

feeling of doom, fearing that I might not be looking at them much longer. I sat on the banks of a dike and pondered on the unpremeditated career I had chosen for myself. Would I get a job in a newspaper office? Would I be able to learn shorthand and typing? If so, where? The sun inched its way slowly down towards the horizon, staring at me from behind a cluster of brickyard chimneys now in silhouette. At least I would not be spending my life *there*. I watched the smoke smearing the sky and thought of the days when father worked for the London Brick Company. I remembered the times I had visited him on his kiln and how he had lifted me up to look over the wall so that I could see the distant lights of Peterborough. Would I be going there after all? Surely, if my father had been given the chance when he was a young man he would have chosen something better. But he'd had no choice in the matter. He had taken what work there was. For me it was different.

It was a very quiet evening. No traffic passed. I sat alone with only the sounds of the fields, which were almost silent. It was so quiet I felt I could hear the sun ticking, minute by minute as I contemplated my uncertain future. What would my father decide?

By suppertime he had made up his mind. He was prepared to send me to a private Commercial School in Peterborough where I could learn the skills necessary for my future. 'You won't be going back to Station Road any more ... Your mother will take you through to Peterborough in the morning to see if they'll have you. If so, you can start next week.'

'But what about my summer holidays.'

He scoffed. 'There's gratitude for you. You can forget all about summer holidays, young man. You're like the rest of us now. You'll have what you can afford. If I'm prepared to spend my hard-earned money on your education you will blinking well have to work for it too.'

That, I suppose, was the moment between two seasons when everything changed. Not only was it a break with family traditions in that I was *not* expected to become another manual worker, but I was no longer a child. I was now a young man with a responsibility. The generous hours of freedom had come to an end. Childhood was over.

By the end of the week I was enrolled in Mrs Bean's

Commercial School in the Cathedral Precincts. She already looked old, Victorian, and very superior. She was running the school in the absence of her son who was still in the Services. There was, I think, some hesitation on her part before I was accepted. 'Most of my pupils, of course, are girls. I have only ten boys and feel sometimes they are more trouble than they are worth. I shall need a good reference from your present headmaster and one other reliable person. I shall also want a promise from you that you will work hard. Boys are notoriously lazy.'

There were one or two problems to sort out before I could start. Permission had to be granted by the Isle of Ely Education Committee, or Cambridgeshire Education Authority, for me to leave the senior boys school a term early and my headmaster was not very willing to let me go. 'You should finish your time here properly before seeking further education. Your father is being unreasonable. It won't cost him any more to make you wait.' Not directly, I tried to explain. It simply meant that I'd be that much later in getting a job and earning money. My father could not afford to keep me that long.

Whatever objections there were must have been sorted out fairly quickly because I did not return to Station Road, or have the chance of saying 'goodbye' to my teachers or class-mates. The next thing I knew was that I was on the 8.25 a.m. bus, ready to face my first day at a new school. I felt conspicuous with my new satchel which contained a Collins dictionary, pencil-case, and my packed lunch. Most of the seats on the bus were occupied by other boys (and girls) going to *their* schools, some to Fletton grammar school, others to the King's School or the County grammar school, and a few to the Commercial School. The boys were quick to see the pristine condition of my satchel and decided to hurl it up and down the gangway until they were stopped by the bus conductress.

Twenty minutes later we pulled up in Bridge Street, disembarked and rushed, or dawdled, to wherever our days would be spent. The route was to become a very familiar one, passed Morley's the pawnbrokers, Sturton's the chemists, Macfisheries, Woolworths, the City Cinema, Polyfotos, the Zip Cleaners, Marks and Spencer, the Angel Hotel,

Woodcock's cafe, Freeman Hardy and Willis, the billiard hall above Burtons and, finally crossing the road to enter the cathedral precincts through the Norman gateway. Despite my fears, I managed to pause for a moment to look up at the great west front of the cathedral, a building which I had yet to enter.

Opposite the commercial school was the cathedral Song School where the choristers were already rehearsing the day's services. It was a wonderful, ethereal sound, unlike any singing I had heard. If that was the kind of music I would be greeted by each morning then I would not mind attending school for another year.

Two other boys started with me that day, one from Yaxley and one from March. We entered the classroom like a trio of sheep, each afraid to speak first in the presence of so many girls. Mrs Bean had not yet arrived so we were taken in by the deputy headmistress, a tall, elegant young woman whose sophistication only partly masked her impatience with us. We could see on her brow the signs of despair – 'Oh no, not three more peasants from the fens! Can't they find work for them on the land these days?' She rose imperiously from her desk, stepped towards us like a model from a fashion magazine and said, 'Well? And what are you three gentlemen here for? All planning to become company secretaries, no doubt, or chartered accountants? Hmm? Or are you aiming for something higher? Chancery, perhaps, or Whitehall? I can tell you one thing for a start. You will all have to look considerably smarter than you do now. Just look at those dreadful knots in your ties. Where did you sleep last night – in a haystack? And your hair! Look at it. When do you propose to get a decent haircut? Hmm? People who enter the professions must look professional, even if they are not. I can see we have a great deal of work to do on you all. What do you think, girls?' She turned to the rest of the class who were enjoying this performance. 'Go to that table at the back of the room and pay attention. I will sort out your timetable at break.'

We did as we were told and sat in silence as she continued with her lesson on double entry bookkeeping. We noticed there were two other boys in the class but they only glanced at us sympathetically as we passed. When I saw the columns of figures on the board and words like *debit, credit,* and *balance,* my heart sank.

If bookkeeping was a mystery, shorthand was an obscure and foreign language we knew we would never learn in ten years, let alone in one or two. We stared at the rows of strange hieroglyphs as they were drawn on the board and obediently repeated the sounds they represented – *puh ... buh ... chuh ... kuh ... muh ... nuh ... inn ... ing ...* and so on. Having recently become interested in Egyptology I said, in knowing tones to the boy from Yaxley, 'It's just like Egyptian. We shall need a Rosetta stone to unravel those scrawls.'

The teacher heard me and called me to the front of the class. 'Now, young man, perhaps you will let us all share in your little secret. What did you say?'

I blushed and did not reply. 'Come on', she insisted, 'tell us what you said.'

I told her and she looked astonished that I could know anything about Egypt. 'I can see you are one of those boys who blush every time they're found out. I like boys who blush. They can never tell lies with any conviction, can they!'

She began to straighten my tie. 'You see, you are blushing even more. Is it because you are embarrassed to have a lady trying to make you look smart?'

I could smell her perfume. Our bodies were almost touching. I now felt myself going scarlet. I had never been so close to such an attractive woman. She smiled. 'You could be quite a nice young man, when you have learnt how to behave properly and dress decently. Go back to your place.'

Although she continued to humiliate me for the rest of that term I couldn't help liking her. She had poise, flair, a lovely figure – and could be witty as well as sarcastic. I am sure she had picked on me because she thought she could help. I was not a good pupil and she had every right to get angry with me on many occasions. I may not have been the instigator of each crime but was usually the first culprit to get caught. Setting fire to a girl's hair was unintentional but I *did* throw the match across the room. Flooding the cloakrooms was not deliberate but I *had* been party to blocking the overflows. Putting my foot through the top of a table was *not* an act of vandalism but just *bad* luck. Admittedly I was dancing on it at the time but I thought it was made of sterner stuff than that. Every afternoon in winter the boys had to put up the blackouts (which were still in use) so that the classroom lights could be switched on. Although the war was nearly over restrictions still existed and we made the most of this duty, disrupting the class for several minutes as we clowned about. We missed being expelled by the narrowest of margins, *or* divine intervention.

The teacher I enjoyed working for most was the one who took us for typing and English. She was interested in music and drama and on a few occasions invited me to see some of the local amateur productions in which she was acting. I took easily to typing, no doubt because my fingers had already acquired a certain dexterity through years of playing the piano. I achieved a reasonable speed without having to stare at the keys and managed to pass one or two RSA examinations. It was about the only skill I learnt at school which was to prove useful in the career I finally settled for, enabling me to do most of my own typing. Some shorthand remained and that, in fact, helped me to get my first job, but lack of use eventually led to it becoming as obsolete as a foreign language never spoken after leaving school. I was not sorry to give up Pitman's *Shorthand Journal* so that the money could be spent on something else, such as a visit to the Odeon or Broadway Kinema, or a *risque* copy of *Men Only*, though the change did not take place immediately. What was changing was the pace of life. It might sound amusing now but after the slow tempo of life in Whittlesey, the whirl of activities in Peterborough (which was then a quiet cathedral city) was a stimulating contrast. I began to see myself more as a city boy than a fen boy and did not realize how, for a few years, I was to lose touch with all my former associations. I began to feel a stranger in my own town.

11   Be careful with your change
and mind the dogs

Although much smaller than it is today, Peterborough then had an identity of its own and retained the parochial air of a market-town. Its narrow streets were made up mainly of family businesses where tradesmen still lived above the shop and the city centre did not become a ghost town after dark. The market-square in front of the Guildhall was cobbled and we had markets twice a week. The stalls, with their coloured awnings, spilled over into the streets and the stall-holders brought their own racy patter in order to attract customers.

Market days helped to brighten up a city that was still suffering from wartime drabness. Air-raid shelters had been erected down the centre of Bridge Street and in the cathedral precincts; shops did not always have much stock to display in the windows, which were still gum-taped against bomb blast, and there were always long queues at the fishmongers' and butcher's shops. Some of the premises had also been taken over as Servicemen's clubs or rest-rooms, which attracted a lot of Americans on leave with a ready supply of money, gum and nylons, and we found ourselves completely outclassed when it came to chatting-up girls.

One of the brightest attractions of the city then was its cinemas. During the war years an average of 27 million people went each week 'to the pictures'. As Peterborough had a choice of picture-palaces we could have gone to several times a week – had funds allowed. There was the City Cinema, the Odeon, the Princess, the Broadway Kinema, the New England, and the Savoy. In addition to films there were lively variety shows at the Embassy and a resident repertory company (called the Court Players) at the Empire Theatre.

None of them survives today. During those years the two theatres alone offered a good variety of entertainment. At the Embassy we could see Elsie and Doris Waters or Vic Oliver, and at the Empire we could have a play by Oscar Wilde, Somerset Maugham or J.B.Priestley. Before the theatre was pulled down we had even progressed to plays by Terence Rattigan and Arthur Miller.

I had never been a regular cinema-goer as a child and only occasionally went to a Saturday matinee at the Super Cinema in Whittlesey when there was a Roy Roger's movie. I went more often in the evenings with my mother who, unlike father, enjoyed a good film and took me along for company. As much as the films themselves I loved sitting in the dimly lit stalls waiting for the shimmering curtains to open. As the audience came in we listened to the music of Victor Sylvester and watched Miss Siggie – the oldest usherette in the business – bullying late-comers to their seats. Then the final moment of anticipation as the lights went down, the screen-curtains opened, and a beam from the projection-room flickered through the darkness to transport us into a world of make-believe. The programme changed halfway through the week so the towns people had the chance of seeing two main features and two B-movies each week. One of the first films I saw has stayed in my memory because of its sound-track. It was the music of *Die Fledermaus* and I think the film might have been called *The Bat*, though I can't trace it now. It was about a conductor and there were several scenes of him conducting an orchestra, which increased my ambition to achieve similar fame. There was also *The Song of Bernadette* which made my mother weep copiously and say, on the way home, 'It was worth every penny.' By the time I became a cinema-goer in Peterborough my taste had changed and I preferred something a little more meaty, not that the film industry had anything like the freedom it has now. I can remember how people queued for hours to see the first 'X' movie that came to the city, which was Jane Russell in *The Outlaw*. There were protests in the streets and sermons from the pulpits about such a degrading film being allowed on our screens. There was a similar outcry when *Forever Amber* came but it only succeeded in lengthening the queues. But the prize for the longest queue seen outside a local cinema must go to *Gone with the Wind*. People had to wait so long to see that epic that they took flasks of tea, coffee, and packs of sandwiches with them.

Not only did Peterborough have its cinemas to attract but there were also book-shops, music shops, a museum, library, cafes, parks, and boats on the river. So, to move each morning from a town with a population of 8,000 to a city which then had 58,000 was, for a boy of fourteen, an alluring experience which naturally made him forget about the simpler joys at home.

The cathedral was also a place that I was to enjoy once I had overcome my fear of it. Although I saw it every day as I went to school it was to be several weeks before I found the courage to go inside, especially alone. My first two visits were with other boys at the school and were not always made with the reverence we should have shown. We came close to getting in trouble more than once and the head verger at that time took a particular dislike to us, with good reason. He blamed us if the fires went out in the Victorian stoves, if a chair was found to be broken we must have vandalized it, and if someone put chewing-gum in the offertory box it must have been one of us. Sometimes his suspicions and complaints were justified. One morning some of the boys climbed down into the crypt and lit small fires with pages torn from their exercise-books, not to cause harm but to find their way around the dark underground passages. When one of the assistant vergers saw smoke escaping from a ventilation grille he raised the alarm. The boys were found, hauled back to school and suspended for two weeks. One of the boys, an impish Irish lad from Yaxley, had more devil in him than most and once accepted bets from the rest of us that he dare not climb to the top of the cathedral up some scaffolding that had been erected at the east end for repair work. With the agility of a monkey he made his way up to the tower, his triumphant shouts only faintly heard from such a height, but loud enough to attract attention from one of the clergy who swiftly took the matter in hand and told Mrs Bean that she must never let us near the place again.

During the summer months most of us took packed lunches so that our pocket-money could be spent on hiring a boat on the River Nene. We hired our boats from Jack

Hammond, whose landing-stage was then near the customs house. He came to know us well and let us take out some of his best craft, which was a greater risk than he could have appreciated.

'You don't need a rudder if you row properly', shouted John Kelly. 'Pull it in ...'

'Why don't we row in pairs', suggested Nutty Slack, 'then we'll all get a turn with the oars much quicker.'

The boat rocked and lurched and we changed places. It did not worry us that out of the four or five only two could swim. Water came over the sides and once we rocked so much that we lost both oars and were left to float helplessly downstream. Fortunately another boat came to the rescue and Jack Hammond gave us a jolly good ticking-off when he heard about our behaviour.

Because I enjoyed rowing so much I often went on my own after school for an hour. I always rowed away from the town, going downriver towards Whittlesey, content to feather the oars gently over the placid water or drift with only the sound of the river lapping the bows. This was a new freedom, a different kind of stillness, and a new view of the fens. I had always enjoyed walking along riverbanks and liked watching herons. Now I found I could slide much closer to them. They became an obsession. It was through them that I began to see how everything is related to its local habitat. The herons were not just grey. Their greyness was a colour that came out of that landscape of clay-pits and brickyards. So when I came to write about them later I wanted to place them in that world –

> Clay-grey the scraggy heron haunts
>   the narrow waters of the Nene,
> half-bird, half-spirit, now he stands
>   quiet as the grass or waiting stones ...
>
> And if I move or make a sound,
>   with ghost-like wings he floats away,
> a stretch of river-bank in flight,
>   a heavy shadow from the sky.

Such experiences soon tempted me back to my home-town and the 'city boy' gladly surrendered to the former pleasures of going out into the fens on his own. Ignoring my homework

I cycled again to Black Bush, Glassmoor Bank, Chapel Bridge and Cock Bank, where I was able to appreciate more than ever that the fields were no longer just fields, or the farms just farms. They were all part of a unique landscape – a mostly man-made landscape. They were now even *more* than just a landscape. They were becoming the source of my whole being. I had always enjoyed the vast open spaces of the fens and the great dome of sky under which we lived, but now I wanted to know what was at their beginning. What was there before the crops, before the plough, before the first footprint? Where did each river start? Where did it go? Why were our rivers straight, the soil so black? I loved to watch the evening mist transform the land and it was on such a night that I wrote my first poem about the fens –

> I ride through a kingdom of mist
> where farms drown in a phantom sea
> and May piles up in the hedge like snow
> waiting to melt in tomorrow's sun.

And I can remember how, as I turned for home, that the mist had also made the town disappear, that I had to find a safe harbour by instinct. I felt excited to think that I was the only person who could see this, that –

> night comes down where day once grew,
> lights ripple through this thin white sea,
> while in the village children sleep
> never to know they slept in sky.

The scale of my landscape was important, so too were its moods. Sometimes everything was diminished by it and made to seem insignificant. At other times the vastness made insignificant things look majestic. A bare tree against a fenland sky is no more than an enlargement of the veined and transparent leaf it has shed. A rainbow does have a beginning and an end as it arches over the land. A sod of peat is no more than a remnant of some ancient forest but, held in the hand and smelt, it becomes the essence of those long-forgotten woods. If the landscape had an identity, then everything within that landscape had to have its own identity as well, however small. All things were related. I began also to appreciate just how much influence light and space had on the world around me. No two days were alike. No two skies were ever the same. Some days the sky looked as if it slumped like an unmade bed on the horizon. On other days it stretched so high, so skin-tight above us, that we expected it to burst into a more dazzling world beyond. Images began to form in my mind without my knowing what a poetic image was. All I knew then was that such a landscape could not be adequately described within a language that was still, for me, inarticulately earthbound. Perhaps only music could portray its beauty but I knew that my limited talent in that art could never match the challenge. So how was I to make permanent these moments that now excited me? The camera could not do it, nor the artist's brush. Perhaps this elusive, intangible quality must forever remain secret, and personal.

Back at school, and with winter approaching. I was no longer content with a packed lunch and wanted to join most of the other boys who now went to a fish restaurant in Cumbergate each day. My father said I could do the same but I would have to earn my own dinner-money. I had long been aware that my money supply was considerably less than the other pupils at school, whose parents were clearly better off and could afford to give them more. So I got a job as an errand-boy with a family-butcher in our street who was prepared to pay me five shillings a day. I started work each Saturday morning at eight o'clock and finished at five or six in the evening. It was a hard day and, by the time I returned home, I believed I was one servant worthy of his hire.

My first round was always made up for me by Charlie, one of the butcher's sons, who had not been called up into the war like his brothers. He lifted the heavy basket of meat on to my trades-bike, told me which streets to do first, then saw me off the premises with a word or two of advice. 'Be careful with your change and mind the dogs.' From that moment I was on my own.

I looked at the clean white enamel tray on which I carried the portions of rationed meat to each customer, then at the leather pouch containing the five shillings worth of change which had to balance with the rest of the takings at the end of the day, and went from house to house without knowing one joint of meat from another. I could tell the difference between liver and sausages but that was all. The meat had often been kept in a refrigerator for weeks and, to my eye, looked a sad, uniform grey. When one customer asked, 'Where did this come from – the morgue?' I simply replied, 'I suppose so.' and waited for the money.

The first hour determined the mood of the day. If I fell off the bike – and the unwrapped portions of meat were strewn over the ground – I was in a temper for the rest of Saturday. If I got off to a good start, I enjoyed my rounds and gave each customer a friendly smile as I handed over the week's offering of pork or lamb. In fact, it was never called lamb in those uncertain days but mutton – or 'jump-dyke' as my mother always described it. Lamb was something the rationing of meat never allowed, as far as I could make out. Gradually I began to tell the difference between one animal and another and spoke with some authority when anyone asked in tones of disbelief, 'You call that pork? It looks more like newly-mixed cement.' Or, 'Are you sure this ain't horseflesh?'

I enjoyed calling at so many houses, where I was often asked inside while the customer searched high and low for the money which had been put somewhere safe. Then I was able to stare round all the paraphernalia that other people gathered round their lives. Each house had its own peculiar smell. Some smelt of pipe-smoke and Brasso, some of rain and geraniums, others of dry-rot and mothballs, some of babies and cooking. Week after week I grew accustomed to the smell and sights of each home. With some it was the furniture, with others the pantries, or the sinks, or cats. I got to know the calendars, plants, ornaments and knick-knacks as well as I knew those in my own front room.

The customers were no less interesting than their houses. Some were always grumbling, some constantly cheerful, some quite eccentric. I suppose the one who stands out most is the old man who lived in a black tarred wooden bungalow where there was no point in wiping your feet on the doormat as you went in because your shoes were likely to be dirtier coming out. There was often sheets of newspaper on the floor which, as it was explained to me, were put there 'to help keep the place tidy' but they clearly failed. It was no surprise when I discovered one day that he kept chickens in his bedroom.

On the Saturday that I called his wife was out shopping and he was ill in bed. He shouted out, 'Come on in!' I found my way through to the bedroom and was a little startled to see a magnificent cockerel sitting on the brass rail at the foot of his bed. I thought we had kept fine cockerels at home but this one had the dignity of an Egyptian pharaoh.

'I can see you like my old cockerel', said the man with a chuckle. 'Sits there all day long, lazy old davvil. Lovely creature, though. Feel his crop! Goo on, 'e won't 'urt yer.'

I stretched my hand towards the bird and asked the man, 'What happens to him at night?'

'He stays where he is, of course. The missis ain't too fond on 'im but 'e's comp'ny for me. Anything's company where you're old.'

A few weeks later the man died on the Friday afternoon before I called on the Saturday. His wife insisted that I should go through to see him. The blinds were drawn. The room in semi-darkness. A jug and basin stood on the table and a half-full chamberpot with a broken handle was on the chest of drawers. I looked at the bed and there was the thin, blind, stone face of the man, barren and expressionless as a frozen pond, his nostrils stuffed with cotton-wool, his bald head like a pebble in the sand of his soiled pillow. I looked at the foot of the bed and then at the old man's wife. 'Where's the cockerel?'

'Oh, he's gone too ... I wrung 'is neck last noight and buried 'im near the rhubbub ... I couldn't 'ev stayed 'ere with 'im still alive, bless 'im, or eaten 'im. 'E were too much the other 'alf of my poor old mate. No, they both 'ad to goo.'

She began to cry and I withdrew from the room, not bothering to enter in my notebook whether she had paid or not. As I cycled away I couldn't help wondering what would have happened if the cockerel had died first.

What my Saturday rounds did teach me was that there was a lovely, warm, generous quality about so many of these people. Their lives were, it is true, often narrow and basic. They did not allow themselves many luxuries, nor did they believe that they needed them. One couple – a brother and sister – lived alone in a poor house, lop-sided with subsidence and damp. Because one end of the house was lower than the other its roof gave the appearance of an animal lying there with a broken back. The woman had once been in service and was then skilled in embroidery and playing the piano. Her young man had been killed in the First World War and she had never found anyone else. Her brother was a bachelor and had lived with his parents all his life, working on the same farm as his father. When they died he was unable to keep the house tidy, so his sister gave up her own house to go and look after him. It was a meagre existence for her. They spent their years by the same fire, encamped in their separate corners of a miserable room, putting one piece of coal on at a time, twiddling time round their thumbs until the oil-lamp told them it was time for bed. The sadness was that the woman was reduced to the poverty around her and had no resolve to improve matters.

One customer always greeted me like a prodigal son and invited me into his living-room where he cut me a thick slice of home-cured ham to eat while he counted out his money from an Oxo tin to pay for his meat. 'I don't know why I buy this bloody rubbish from the butcher's when I can produce ham like that, do you!' The table was always laid and the cloth did not look as if it had been shaken for a few days. The milk stayed in its bottle and the plates remained unwashed until there were enough 'to justify boiling the kettle.'

When my morning rounds were done I went home for a quick lunch, then returned to help Charlie with the out-of-town rounds in the afternoon, which we did by van. This was always a pleasure in summer for we frequently stopped to buy an ice-cream or bottle of lemonade. But in winter it was different. The fens are quick to change their character. What was once bounteous and benign suddenly became bleak and forbidding. More than once we found ourselves out in a November fog where most of the familiar landmarks had disappeared. Not all fenland roads are straight. The more ancient ones follow what used to be tracks over the marshes before the fens were drained. Others make their way along the routes of old forgotten rivers. But, whether roads are straight or winding, they can be awfully perplexing in fog.

The worst experience we had was the day when our van kept breaking down. We were already an hour late with our deliveries and the winter daylight had not long to go before darkness took over. Suddenly it went very quiet and the wind dropped. Then, slowly, out of the fields came a thick grey mist, heaving and breathing like a living thing – a silent, impenetrable wall like a tidal wave in slow motion. It engulfed us. Within minutes we were lost, not knowing which way to turn even though it was a route we took each week.

'This is all we want', said Charlie. 'God knows what time of night we shall get home now. You'd better hang your head out of the window to see where we are going. Shout if you see anything in the way, like a dike or tree.'

We made our way as if driving through a minefield. The fog draped itself like frayed wool over the bonnet of the Austin van. It stuck to my hair and eyebrows. Its wet, furry, burnt-out smell caught in my throat. If there had ever been anything beyond the fog, it now ceased to exist. The only sound in the world was of our van chugging along the road. Even straight roads can deceive you into thinking there is a bend and we swerved from one side of the road to the other. Suddenly the van jerked and jolted over some potholes. Then it coughed, spluttered and stopped. If a van can ever have anything like a death-rattle, that was it.

Charlie pushed his cap to the back of his head, mopped his brow and swore. When we got out to see what had happened we discovered that we were stranded on a railway level-crossing, which wasn't very level. Nothing appeared to be broken on the van and we had not run out of petrol. But we were stuck. 'Well, we've got to get this damn thing off the line' Charlie said, 'even though it's unlikely that there'll be any trains running in this weather.'

We pushed and heaved until the van was clear of the crossing and then Charlie got the cranking handle to see if he could get any life out of the engine. He swung the handle round several times but there was not a flutter or response. 'Give it a bit more choke', he called. After a few more attempts there was the gasp and shudder of something very old waking up. 'Got it, the old bugger!' he said with relief. He hurried back into the driver's seat and we drove away. It was now very dark as well as foggy and it was only when we reached the outskirts of the town that we began to recognize dimly the outlines of familiar buildings.

Still saddle-sore from my morning round, and now hand-chapped, red-eyed, cold and weary from the afternoon, I went home, flopped into a chair by the fire, too tired to say a word. My five shillings had been well and truly earned that day. 'Well?' said mother. 'Aren't you going to explain where you've been until this time of night?' I was too exhausted to explain. 'Go and ask Charlie', I said, and closed my eyes.

It was a relief to us all when winter was over. Four years of war, of food-rationing, blackouts and fuel shortages, were beginning to demoralize even those who had not been otherwise affected by the hostilities. Spring still had the power to rejuvenate and,now that we had 'double summer time" to allow longer daylight hours – both for work and the Allied bombers, the days from March to October had an extra bonus. I could spend more of my time out of doors and now enjoyed walking over the washlands towards the River Nene and North Side. This, too, may have been because of my growing uncertainty as to where I now belonged – the city, or the fens. It was a kind of no man's land between two frontiers. From The Dog-in-a-Doublet inn I could see, on the western boundary, the distant lights and landmarks of Peterborough, while to the north and east I was still in touch with the familiar landscape of black soil, dykes, bulrushes and reeds – and, yes, the ghosts of ancestors.

The road between Whittlesey and Thorney had always been a favourite walk with our family before the war. There was little traffic then and, in summer-time, my parents often took us for a stroll over the Wash as far as the Nene Bridge. There they would have a drink at either The Swan, or The Dog while we sat outside on a wooden bench sipping lemonade and eating crisps. It was not unusual for friends and relatives to be doing the same thing and there would be long periods of conversation among the adults while the children went down the bank to be near the river. Beyond the washlands were the ubiquitous brickyard chimneys smudging the sky, and towards the town we could still see the tall spire of St Mary's church like a compass needle to guide us all back home.

These washlands, used mainly for grazing, were the same that we had seen in winter under floodwater or ice. But in summer they were transformed into a paradise of wildlife.

Grass shimmered with buttercups, Willow trees were now bouncy with new growth. Swans glided along Morton's Leam. The sky was a canopy of lark song. Hares leapt across dykes and, because the washlands were never ploughed in those days, they had their own smell – a cool, damp, honey smell of clover, trefoil, fern – and cows.

Now, as a teenager, I found the road a convenient link between one way of life and another, between the present and the past. The child I had been was already a shadow. Were those fields beginning to lose their glory? Was I now looking for something beyond their fading innocence?

This first feeling of breaking away from home was intensified by the death of my grandfather who had meant so much to me as a child. He had been ill for many weeks and died on 4 September 1944, a few days before his seventy-eighth birthday. I have to admit that I did not feel much sorrow at the time. As a fourteen-year-old boy my own life was too full and important to be affected by this expected loss. It was only years later that I became aware of what he meant to me. The day of his funeral was warm. We gathered at my Aunt Daisy's house (where my grandparents lived) and I can remember upsetting my father by some callous remark I made when the hearse arrived. My father and I were going through a phase (which was to be a prolonged one) of never quite understanding each other. The cars made their solemn way to the chapel for the funeral service and then back to the cemetery for the burial. There was much weeping and I was at an age when I could not appreciate such grief. I had forgotten what a kind, gentle person my grandfather had been, how he had fetched my medicine and pills from the doctor's surgery, how he had sat by my bedside for hours on end, how he had encouraged me with my music. I think I was in my thirties before his death finally 'got to me' and I then wrote a poem in his memory, which ended with the lines, 'Only now / years later in a cramped city, can I / be grateful for his influence and love.' Since then I do not think there is a week, or even a day, goes by without him coming into my thinking.

1945–90

12   Roads whose routes are not on maps

1945 was a momentous year. Adolf Hitler and his mistress committed suicide. The hideousness of the Nazi concentration camps shocked the world. The German Army surrendered to the Allied Forces at Montgomery's headquarters on Luneberg Heath, and the German Supreme Command surrendered at Rheims. The war in Europe was over. Now, we thought, life could get back to normal. But life never is normal after a war and the world of post-1945 was to be very different from the one of pre-1939. Values change. Revised attitudes emerge. Having survived we believe that at least we have the chance to build something new out of the ruins of the old. It must have been the same after the Plague and the Great Fire of London. We thought it possible after the 1914-18 war. Now, once again, we could plan a safer life in a better world. Slogans! And often the slogans for peace are as trite as the slogans for war, with a political shallowness about them rather than philosophical conviction. In our eagerness to make a new start we usually throw out the good with the bad and only appreciate what we have lost when it is too late.

But there was justification for our uninhibited joy in celebrating a return to peace and VE Day gave the nation a long-awaited opportunity to go mad, get drunk, kiss the neighbour's wife, wave flags, ring bells, blaze lights into the dark and, for a moment, forget the dead. Now we could chop up the blackout shutters, uncork the bottles of home-made wine, bring out the faded bunting and dance through the night. I helped father to nail a large Union Jack on to a clothes'-prop which we then hung from our front bedroom window. The Christmas-tree fairy lights were shaped into a V on the wall outside and the radio volume turned up to compete with the rest in our row. Street parties were

organized and children stood around bewildered and amused
to see the grown-ups behaving so recklessly. Neighbours
went from house to house collecting food, drinks, tables,
chairs, cups, plates, spoons, forks and tea-cloths for a party
which looked as if it was going to last all year. Trestle-tables
were erected along the length of the street. Wooden forms
were borrowed from the Salvation Army and Methodist
schoolrooms. Jars of home-made cider took their place with
the teapot, dandelion-and-burdock, ginger beer and orange
squash. Pianos were pushed out on to the pavements,
radiograms brought out from dusty corners and placed near
the doors. There were so many noises and tunes that we
forgot that the church bells were ringing for the first time
after their long silence.

As the parties got going the children soon joined in,
fighting for cream buns, trifles, jellies and salmon
sandwiches. Cups of tea were knocked over, glass tumblers
broken, accidents happened and minor miracles were
performed. Some of the older girls cartwheeled, or walked on
their hands, displaying their knickers to the whistling men.
Boys went in for obstacle races that included going through
baths of slimy water, eating toffee-apples suspended from
lengths of string, and jumping the last lap home in
potato-sacks. There was a fancy dress parade, in which most
of the younger children found themselves made up as
something resembling Winston Churchill, Britannia, a
chimney-sweep or walking pillar-box. Hours did not matter,
nor did work. This day was to celebrate a return to peace. As
daylight faded and the evening took over, people began
dancing in the streets and, for quite a few, the effects of too
much drink could no longer be disguised. There were bonfires
on patches of waste-ground and the flames added their own
uninhibited joy to the night sky. I wanted to be in two places
at once – in my own street with all our neighbours and in the
rest of the town where similar parties were in full swing. I
could not resist the temptation to go and see those
celebrations on a larger scale and walked up to the
market-place. A large crowd had formed itself into a gyrating
pattern of rings as everyone sang 'Knees up Mother Brown'
or the 'Hokey-Cokey', It was tribal, pagan, hypnotic and
quite irresistible. A woman of about forty grabbed me by the

arm and pulled me into the ring. 'Come on in, me duck and join us … You won't get hurt with me around … I'll look after you … Oooh, you are lovely!' And she gave me a crushing squeeze. Her bare arms fastened around me and my arms reached involuntarily about her waist. 'My! You're a fast learner', she said. 'Proper little heart-throb … Do you by any chance have an older brother?' I did not like the smell of her body and when the crowd changed direction to go round the ancient buttercross the other way, I slipped from her grasp and looked for a different group of revellers.

It was well past midnight before the celebrations began to die down. Gradually, two by two, men and women drifted off into a Noah's ark of darkness. Drunks propped each other up in the road. The bells stopped ringing. Streets became quiet. Behind closed doors and curtained windows, those who had paid more dearly for this victory lamented, or rejoiced, in their own private way. I looked up at St Mary's church spire, then across to the parish hall, and thought of the young men who would never come back. Could such wild rejoicing also be a mourning? It was, of a kind. A death, more than an uncertain beginning.

I walked back to my own street. Only a solitary man sat in the middle of our debris, playing his concertina. I listened to the disjointed music and recognized the irony of the tune 'There's no place like home …' It was the final trick of the nightmare. It felt like the end of the world – the last, grey, smoky, tired, spent-out whisper of longing and regret.

I still could not take myself indoors. Instead I walked back down the street, beyond the chapel and the pubs, beyond the river and the railway-lines, away from the tawdry lights and dying bonfires of the town, until I stood in the silent darkness of the fens. Above me the ancient constellations regained their authority. The fields and stars had seen it all before. This was reality. All the rest I had seen that night had been unreal, a crazy pantomime or dream which was already over. The earth, which I could feel but not see, was constant, everlasting, and quietly waiting for daylight.

Suddenly tired and depressed I walked back home, opened the back door which had been the backcloth of many of our family photographs, drank a glass of water, turned out the light and went upstairs to bed. As I crept through my parents' bedroom my mother said, 'You're late!'

'I've been for a walk, down Ramsey Road.'

'On your own?'

'Yes.'

'You'd better get some sleep ...'

My brother was already fast asleep so I sat by the small window of my room, looked again over the roof-tops of the town, and suddenly felt very grown up. Although I would not be fifteen until my next birthday there was little fear of being out alone on such nights, no threat of violence or the unknown. Not that I was allowed to stay out late very often. My parents usually wanted me in the house by half-past nine and some of the worst rows I had with them were because this rule was broken. It was not wilful defiance but a reluctance to separate myself from the deep mysterious space of night.

The winter that ended this eventful year was a particularly bleak one. Food was still rationed, the weather was too cold, not even Christmas could relieve earth's cheerlessness for long. Now that I was no longer a child much of the season's attraction had gone. There were no more pillow-cases to hang at the foot of the bed, no more stars of wonder to fill the expectant skies. I went out carol-singing with the chapel choir, made up mostly of cousins, and we tried to keep ourselves warm by carrying hot potatoes in our pockets and sipping flasks of tea laced with rum. We called at houses where we knew we would get mince-pies and a glass of sherry or port. We trudged arm-in-arm through the snow and watched our breath turn silver in the frosty air. We sang our messages of peace on earth and goodwill towards men, and then went home. But something had changed, or was changing. There would be few surprises on Christmas Day, no family parties, and I think I was already beginning to experience that wish to get the whole thing over with so that we could get back to normal. That dispiriting affliction – teenage boredom – was threatening. It was an ailment I had never known, did not like or believe in, and I was determined not to give in. I may not have been hyperactive but I was not idle either and I hated wasting time. Having outgrown those childhood Christmasses I wanted to get back to doing those things that interested me. I was even prepared to start work. I could see that necessity had its own kind of freedom, releasing me from the restrictions of home. The only trouble was that the more I moved towards the independence of adulthood the sooner I left behind all the things of childhood that I had so much enjoyed. Was it possible to accept the advantages of the one without losing the qualities of the other? Perhaps I was going to be lucky, for I believe writers are among the last people to lose their childlike awareness of life, that essential amazement at the unexpected. I left school not knowing what I was going to do with my newly acquired skills. I could now do 120-words-a-minute in shorthand, was reasonably quick at typing, and had even managed a basic understanding of bookkeeping. But I failed to get a job with either of the two local newspapers I applied to and made no impression at the travel agents who wanted a clerk. I had also failed miserably at the examinations to enter the post office or the electricity board, and a job with a small firm of builders finally went to one of the other boys from the commercial school, a boy who made dullness an art and had been middle-aged since he was five.

In desperation I went to see Mr Gore, the accountant in Whittlesey, who had promised to find me a job when I left school. I arrived at his office in Broad Street, feeling nervous and uncertain as to how I should express, or disguise my present predicament. Surely, after so many rejections, I must be unemployable. He asked me into a room where there was a large desk and a leather chair, which he filled when he sat down. He lit a cigar, played with a large gold ring on his finger, then took out his fountain-pen.

'Can you spell?'

I said I could.

'Reasonably well or very well?'

'Very well I think.'

'And how old are you?'

'Fifteen-and-a-half.'

He puffed a large cloud of smoke into the air. 'Well, I don't need anyone here, you understand, but I might know someone who does. How'd you like to work in a solicitor's office?'

I assured him that it was just the sort of job I was looking for and he disappeared into another room to make a telephone call. While he was out of his office I surveyed the walls. They were tinged with a coat of nicotine and decorated with old prints of racehorses and jockeys. There were several calendars, one for the current year, two for the previous years and one that was ten-years-old. On the shelf were ancient box-files and a pile of ledgers. I was relieved that Mr Gore did not want a junior clerk. His office was too near home, just a few doors from where I had gone to school and less than five minutes from our house.

He came back into the room and gave me a piece of paper on which he had written the name and address of a well-known firm of solicitors in Peterborough. 'D'you know where Priestgate is? That man is a friend of mine and he needs an office boy. It's a good place and you'll be well looked after if you keep your nose clean. You're to go for an interview on Friday afternoon at 2.25. That's the best I can do for you.'

I stood up and thanked him. I knew most of the solicitors' offices in Peterborough and thought them drab, cobwebby places where no sunlight was ever allowed to pry. But the one to which I was sent turned out to be different. The general office was bright and spacious, and four young girls were busy at their typewriters. The receptionist told me to take a seat and I heard my name being announced over the intercom. The walls in this waiting-room were decorated with caricatures of lawyers, judges and courtroom scenes. I wondered if that was what I would look like one day – be-wigged, be-spectacled and with a whisky nose.

A few minutes later I was shown into the senior partner's office. It was palatial, with beautifully bound books lining the walls, two expensive leather armchairs with green velvet cushions, and an imposing oak desk with a silver inkstand and cigarette-box. Behind the desk sat 'C.G.' himself, a tall, impressive, enigmatic man with a considerable reputation as a lawyer in the area – a man who could win two opposing arguments on the same day, as I was to find out.

The interview was brief. I was told that I was being accepted only on the recommendation of Mr Gore because my education was certainly not up to the required standards for such a position, and that I would be on probation for the first six months. My salary would be twenty-two shillings and sixpence a week. If, after that probationary period, I proved to be satisfactory, it would rise to twenty-five shillings.

'If those terms are acceptable to you', said 'C.G.' 'you will start on Monday morning at 8.30 sharp. In the meantime you will get yourself a decent haircut and a three-piece suit, preferably black. You look more like a gipsy at the moment.' He smiled and saw me to the door. 'I hope we shall like each other.'

I woke early that Monday morning, put on a white shirt with a starched collar, my new three-piece suit which I had bought at Burtons on Saturday, and looked at myself in the long mirror of the wardrobe. Yes, the image had changed. I hardly recognized the young man staring back at me. My hair had seldom been as short, nor my shoes so shiny. All I needed now was a rolled umbrella and a briefcase. I was no longer a gipsy, or a peasant. I was about to start on my great career in law. My father had surely not had that in mind when he lifted me on to the wall of the brickyard kiln.

I turned to look out of the bedroom window. It was a bright Reckitt's -blue morning and mother was already busy at her wash-day. At the bottom of the garden was the wash-house, its wake of white smoke unfolding from the chimney. And there was the empty line, sagging, waiting … 'You take your end, I'll take mine … fold and double-fold, don't let go.' Who would help fold the sheets now – my young brother?

I went downstairs, ate my breakfast, went into the garden to say goodbye to my mother, then ran down the street to catch the bus.

'Single, or return?' asked the bus-conductress. It sounded like a death sentence.

For what felt like the whole of my first six months, I glued economy labels on to used envelopes and helped the girl at the reception desk to deal with telephone calls and clients. Each morning I delivered letters to other firms in the city, to save on postage, and, in this way, came to know those boys who were employed in similar jobs. We met, sorted out our letters into districts so that we could deliver them more quickly, then rendezvoused at the Dujon Cafe in Church Street for coffee.

I liked walking round the streets of Peterborough then for it was full of individual and eccentric shops rather than monotonous chain-stores. The smell of newly ground coffee coming from Barber and Ross or Bannister's grocery-shops, the confusion of brasses, belts, straps and harnesses in the saddler's, the apothecarial mysteries of bowls, bottles, pestle and powders in the chemists', all gave the city an atmosphere which only the old can remember. There was a fruiterers' shop in Midgate whose displays of oranges and Brazils were enhanced by notices claiming 'We have the best navels in Peterborough' or 'This is the city's leading nut-shop.' There was the hard-ware store that arranged some of its goods outside the door with a notice saying, 'The Lord helps them that help themselves but God help anybody trying it out here.' And there was the corner newsagents' daring selection of pin-up magazines with hardly a naked bosom in sight. Those were the days when a thigh was erotic and when one newsagent put a magazine in his window revealing the voluptuous breasts of a young woman he was hauled before the magistrates. To walk from Bridge Street, Long Causeway, Midgate, Westgate, Queen's Street and Cowgate was to go on a tour of family businesses which have largely disappeared. There were bespoke tailors, tobacconists, bakers, florists, a china shop and Barrett's departmental store where the change from cashiers flew back on wires across the shop to the waiting customer. Fathers succeeded sons, cheques were accepted without several items of identity or credit cards, and the shop assistant still believed that the customer was always right. One of the few survivors of that class of trader is Brown's the butchers who have kept the traditions and standards alive, enhancing them without having to surrender to the ghetto-blaster and gimmickery of the modern shopping-centre.

As well as the shops there were seven or eight pubs near the market-place, and as many cafes. If we wanted a change from the Dujon, we could go to Woodcocks, Smith's, or the Co-op. There were two Kit-Kat restaurants (which we thought had the tartiest girls) and two British Restaurants – those war-time institutions where you could get a hot meal for one-and-sixpence. We went mostly to the one in Brook Street where the Haig Hall attracted customers from all walks of life – shop-assistants, bus-drivers, market-stallholders, office-workers, teachers, and those whose occupations could not easily be described. There, above the unholy din of dropped trays, clattering utensils, loud music and raucous laughter, we argued about the war, religion, politics and sex. The tables were so close together that it was not possible to have a friendly, intimate discussion. One provocative remark could start people heckling three tables away and soon half the restaurant would be involved. Each plastic chair became a soapbox, each lino-covered table a pulpit.

I became friendly at this time with a young man who was articled to a local firm of architects. Ron was bright and articulate. He preached Socialism with such fervour and eloquence that a revolution seemed the only practical way of solving our economic problems. He sat and argued with men twice his age, men who had been through far worse times and were, no doubt, thoroughly disillusioned. But Ron never gave up. The old system was on its way out. We would have to join hands with our Communist comrades if we were to survive. We were fortunate to be alive at the dawn of this new era ... and so on. Sympathetic though I was, I wondered how long his enthusiasm would last. It was to last far shorter than I could have known.

My friendship with him stemmed from another interest – music. Ron played the saxophone in a local dance-band and collected records to the point of extravagance. He knew all about the big names in the world of popular music – who were the best arrangers, which band had the best brass, who was the greatest soloist. We spent hours in the record-shops listening to the latest issues – Benny Goodman, Louis Armstrong, Tommy Dorsey, Stan Kenton and Harry James. I doubt if I knew Ron more than a year but his influence was to last much longer for I grew to like 'the big band' sound and bought a lot of its music. He left Peterborough for a while and I heard two years later that he had died.

Several other of my friends then were similarly interested in dance bands. One, a trumpet-player, told us that he had a job with a top-class band in London on Saturday nights, but we found out later that he was selling flashy ties from his trumpet-case in Oxford Street. Another took a job as a drummer with Bertrand Mills Circus, and a third, who played the clarinet, volunteered for seven years in the Army and was drowned. So many of my friends were dying in their teens or early twenties that I began to look upon myself as 'the one death missed'.

My own musical interests reverted to brass bands and, increasingly, to the orchestral repertoire. One of the benefits of my job as a solicitor's clerk was that I occasionally got a weekday afternoon off in lieu of working a Saturday morning (for which we did not get paid). This meant that I could leave the office at midday, buy a half-day return to London for seven-and-sixpence, see some of the sights, book a ticket for a concert (also for seven-and-sixpence) and be home by midnight – all for one pound, including refreshments. In this way I was to hear some of my first 'live performances' of music by Prokofiev, Stravinsky and Benjamin Britten and was amazed at what had been happening in the world of music since Mozart and Beethoven. No one could have faced the future with more optimism or enthusiasm. The world was simply a train-journey away.

By the time I was seventeen I thought I had outgrown Whittlesey, that the fens no longer held the attraction for me they once had. That world was now too narrow. I had other interests, other ambitions. I belonged to music clubs and literary societies. I went to music camps and on cycling holidays with my friends. Home was the place to which I returned to sleep when I was nowhere else. I still had to share a bedroom with my younger brother in the same house where I was born but the rest of the family saw little of me. My sister had left home but there were still five of us in that house and I was already running out of space for my collection of books. My youngest brother, Trevor, was now the only child who really needed my parents' attention. I longed for wings
...

They came in a form I did not particularly relish when I was 'called up' for the compulsory stint of national service which most boys had to do immediately after the war. I only just passed the medical examination and was drafted into the RAF. After the initial period of 'square-bashing' I was appointed as a clerical assistant to the camp's medical officer. I had always had a profound aversion to blood but, in my new job, was forced to see plenty of it. Although I had survived the first few months of strenuous training I was eventually declared unfit for military service and discharged. Or, as an uncle always put it, I was "unmedically fit and a liability to the country". The only good thing that came out of that brief episode was the meeting with other young musicians. It was on hearing their talents that I knew my own chances of becoming a professional musician were non-existent. Some of those young men were already very accomplished and one had broadcast on radio. He was a pianist and could make the NAAFI piano sound like a Steinway. Together we were going to write operas which would be performed in Covent Garden. There was no dream beyond our reach. John was also to be discharged as 'unmedically fit' and we both left the station on the same day. "Whatever you do", he said, "don't look back or you'll be turned into a pillar of salt.'

My premature return to civilian life meant searching for another job as I had lost the one at the solicitor's office. Because I had been invalided out of the Services I was now considered a risk by several of the firms that I approached and it was almost out of desperation that I took the job offered to me by a firm of potato merchants in my home-town. This, I felt, was a retrograde step and put me back into a position from which I had recently escaped. But the next six years were to be among the happiest I had known. The firm's offices were in the private grounds of the senior partner – L.C.Giddens – and provided an idyllic setting near the Bower, Black Bush and Ramsey Road. There were trees, formal gardens, lawns and a lovely house right outside my office window and, at the bottom of the garden, a river. There was a touch of irony in this appointment as my father's first job as a houseboy had been at the very same house for a former owner more than forty years ago.

Not only was the work easy, it was also seasonal. Although the three farming brothers between them farmed several thousand acres in the area – which included cattle and cereal crops – their main concern was potatoes. They grew them, bought them off other growers, and sold them to most of the main markets in England, running their own fleet of lorries to deliver them. I began quite early in the morning, helping the senior salesman, Steve Wesley, to phone places like Covent

Garden, Spitalfields, Kidderminster and Brighton. Steve had
already been at work for two hours and usually went home
for his breakfast when I arrived. Buying potatoes off other
growers meant going to the farms to inspect the crops and, in
this way, I was getting to see parts of the fens I had never seen
before. We also went regularly to the family's own farms at
Elm Tree, Yew Tree, Chapel Bridge and Slate Barn. There we
met people whose lives had been spent on the land and they
knew little else. They were warm, forthright characters who
took great pride in their work and believed that what went on
in the rest of the world was no concern of theirs.

As the months passed I could feel the old sap rising, the
stirring of ancient roots, the awareness that I had come back
to where I belonged and I felt at ease. Again, it was the
ordinary things that mattered – the shape of familiar hands,
the smell of an old coat. I could stare into the cold eye of an
indifferent day where mud, mist, furrow and dyke still
reflected the light of an Anglo-Saxon sun. Nothing of any
significance had changed. A man ploughing a field might look
up but hardly notice me there. But that brief acknowledge-
ment would be enough.

Because my office work was easy – and I was usually home
by five o'clock – there were long evenings in which to pursue
my other interests, which now included writing as well as
music. During the summer-time I wrote most of my poems
out of doors, typed them on the office machine the following
day, then sent them off to editors of magazines and BBC
programmes almost before the typewriter had cooled down. I
had beginner's luck and several of those early pieces were
accepted, especially those I had submitted to the BBC
programme *Midland Poets*. I really thought I had arrived.
Then the rejection-slips became more frequent and I soon
found out how much competition there was about.

My discovery of poetry was something of an accident,
anyway, born more out of frustration than desire. I had been
given a seven-and-sixpenny book token for my birthday
which I intended spending on a biography of Tchaikovsky,
already on order at a local bookshop. I waited for weeks and
still it did not arrive so, in desperation, I spent the token on
an anthology of 'Modern Verse'. The deed was done. I
opened its pages and knew that I was in the middle of a

conversion. One poem by Dylan Thomas was enough to send me out into the street with my purchase reading aloud his 'Poem in October'. The phrase "A springful of larks in a rolling cloud" rang through the afternoon like a great surging melody by Elgar or Mahler. Here was music of its own kind and, if I could not compose symphonies, I would settle for poetry. It must have been an unusual sight then for the towns-people to see a young man declaiming poetry down the street but I could not contain my excitement and, from then on, bought as much poetry as I could afford. Most of it was 'modern' from T.S.Eliot to Louis MacNeice and it was only through trying to convince a bookseller in Peterborough that the photograph he had in his shop of Nicholas Blake was, in fact, C.Day Lewis that I was introduced to the poetry of John Clare. I did not know then that Day Lewis was also a crime-writer with a pseudonym and argued fiercely that the caption under the picture was wrong. I remember the ageing man in the shop asking me who C.Day Lewis was and, when I told him that he was a modern poet, he scoffed. "Modern poets! Puh! They are all barbarians. I do hope you also read John Clare?"

I confessed that I did not know who John Clare was and the man shook his head disbelievingly. 'You do not know John Clare? But he is our local poet – lived at Helpston. Greatly underrated, poor chap.'

A poet living in Helpston? Then I must go out to meet him, I said to myself, not knowing that he had died in 1864. The bookseller then showed me the two-volume edition of Clare's poems edited by J.W.Tibble in 1935, which was now 'on sale' for 22s.6d. That was still a week's pay but I bought the books, never dreaming that thirty years later I would write a biography of the 'poor, underrated chap' from Helpston.

By now my eyes had been opened and I knew what I wanted to do. I wanted to write and, furthermore, to write about my own landscape in a way that Clare had written about Northamptonshire. There was no Wordsworthian grandeur in my world, nor was it necessary any more to die of consumption in Rome. But, I still asked myself, was there any poetry in the fens? And what indication was there that the child staring out of that holiday-snap in Heacham in 1933 would ever aspire to write anything in 1950? I was weighed down with doubts.

I look at the photograph again and realize that I do not know that moody boy now any better than I did then. Perhaps we are not the same. Perhaps he is still there, afraid to step out of the waves, or I to step back in. Did the tide ever turn? Does the camera never lie? My father looks the same, and my mother and sister. If I were to go back to that beach would they still be there? In some ways they are, and I am there too – waiting. But so much has happened in between … or, maybe, too little. I do not know which is the real me, or what those distant years mean. 'If all time is eternally present', wrote T.S.Eliot, "All time is unredeemable … What might have been …'

That is always a speculation, a nagging thought that sometimes will not go away. All I know is that 'there was a time' and I was part of it. However innocent that childhood was – innocent, naïve, simple, deprived, blest, which inadequate word do I want? – it was lived in an era when the world went through its own startling period of change. So no other childhood can ever be the same.

Not only was mine different because of the family into which I was born, but also because of the time against which that family had to work out its own existence, even survival. A childhood being lived in the last decade of the twentieth century is bound to be unlike one lived in the third decade. Science, technology, education, social conditions, opportunities and income have all liberated many individuals into making their own choices. It might be argued that such material liberation has not necessarily brought greater freedom. Sophistication is ours at a price. Knowledge is ours at the expense of wisdom. There are other differences too. A childhood that was spent in the fens before the Second World War must be seen in great contrast to one lived since Hitler, Stalin, Auschwitz, Belsen, Hiroshima, the Berlin Wall, Belfast, Saddam and the Gulf – and all the other world events that enter our living-rooms regularly every day. Terrorism, sex, violence, and the daily exposure to the world's problems through the ever-present media, make today's children far more vulnerable and perhaps more cynical than would have been possible fifty years ago. What I can only call 'the world's nakedness' has deprived the young of much of life's wonder and mystery – and this I find sad. They have seen too much history in too short a time. They have been forced to grow up too quickly, both in their families and in the world. There is little security and less love. Survival for them is the game. Innocence belongs to the world of fables, simplicity to some kind of rustic past, naïvety to the uninformed and half-lit. Many modern thinkers may prefer it that way. For all I know, nature itself may equip us for the environment in which we have to survive. Will today's children grow up one day and become nostalgic about their rock music and computor games? Will their memories have a neon-lit aura which belongs to the space age rather than a community? I don't suppose their reminders will be stored in an old shoe-box full of fading photographs. They will be on video and microfilm. In that way they might be more accurate and certainly less quaint. Perhaps they might not even need to remember, to feel they have to belong to somewhere in particular. They will be Time travellers lightly flitting over the earth where only the Present matters. Maybe we each belong to a Time as well as a Place, and make of both what we can.

I have been on a visit to the past and, as another Whittlesey-born author – L.P.Hartley – wrote, "The past is a foreign country." And that is how it feels. What these pages have been concerned about are the beginnings, the discoveries, and the reflections of someone who wanted to know the answers to too many questions. What I have written, both here and elsewhere, can best be summed up in the words of Albert Camus –

> A man's work is nothing but this slow trek to discover through the detours of art those two or three great and simple images in whose presence his heart first opened.

Some of my earliest memories have become the most significant images in my work and however far I might have travelled from those 'great and simple things' the beginnings are the end to which I travel.

> I have been held back by the black walls of love.
> Not love of the breast or the passionate best
> that a woman can give – all this I have;
> but the love of a past that clings to the heels

making it hard to forget all the loving there was.
No bitterness left on the tongue, only regret
for the ills and the pride and all that was wrong.

My father, whose nights were spent on a kiln
turning clay into bricks, fed his fires to burn
at pre-Genesis heat until the heart of the furnace
was Milky-Way white and the stars blind with smoke.
Did his father's ghost ever appear as dawn
broke on those battlements, his footprints in dust?
Light has no brightness like the eyes of truth.

He did not know (nor she who sat by the grate
where coals were already ash and her stars blown out),
that some fires cannot be fed with the breast's milk
or a baker's loaf. Sooner or later the flames grow
restless as Spring at the trees' roots, thrash
like wild waters released from burst banks until
all is consumed in waste and the beast tamed.

There were the walls of a house and a puritan faith
where kindness was wrapped in the wrath of God
and all would be judged, both the good and the bad,
and the fires of hell make the kiln's heat pall.
Fall foul of him, or fall from grace, and we would bake
not for a week or a year but eternity' sake.
(So do not tell me, children, why you weep.)

But who's to blame? Not those who knew no better
than to cry with shame. Whoever thought
of building walls round God made one mistake.
Love is not kept by closing doors, nor bought
with homilies of what we each might owe.
Although my father's ghost said 'you may go',
I could not lose the latch that still locks in.

Not only has that world changed, it has largely disappeared,
or is disappearing more quickly than I once expected. The
brickyards where my father worked have gone, the kiln
reduced to rubble to provide the foundations for factories
making very different things from bricks. The suburb of
King's Dyke itself – those rows of houses where my
schoolfriends and Saturday customers lived – was suddenly

not there any more, wiped off the face of the earth as if hit by a hydrogen bomb. No paths or gardens left to show where people took some pride in growing vegetables. No rooms left in which to display the china cabinets, the plates, the photographs of weddings and grandchildren. The grass, wild and greedy for revenge has taken over every plot as though those homes had never been. Yes, you may say, but many of those people have done better for themselves. Those places needed pulling down. True, the houses in Church Street now are better than the ones which were demolished to make way for them but the street, shops, town and great occasions on the market-place have been reduced to scenes in a one-act play. There comes a time when it is better to inhabit memories.

Is this love of a place, then, simply all in the mind? Did it ever exist? Or has sentiment taken over from truth? It is possible that memory sees the truth through the blurred eyes of nostalgia, especially for anyone who moves a hundred, or thousands of miles away. But six? Surely that distance cannot make one feel an alien, even though my family always managed to make my move to Peterborough sound like a departure to another country. No, six miles cannot sever you from the place of your birth but there is something about crossing boundaries that does make a difference. There was a time (before county boundaries were reorganized) when, going from Whittlesey to Peterborough, we travelled from the Isle of Ely into Northamptonshire, stepping from peat-soil and clay on to limestone. We not only crossed a county boundary, we also crossed a river and a railway-line, both of which separated two worlds from each other. So, 'going home' still meant for me 'going back' across those boundaries, back to the place where everything began, back to those 'great and simple images in whose presence the heart first opened'. There are boundaries too in the mind, experiences which demarcate what we were and what we are. And which wins? For it is a mistake to believe there is no distance between the past and the present.

> There are times when
> the only landscape that satisfies
> is behind closed eyes;
> not the memory of hills
> or a sea's shores, but those

less travelled roads whose
routes are not on maps
but can be traced by contours of a darker
kind ...

This book set out to be mainly about a childhood in the
fens. What I might have said about the topography,
geography and the general history of the area has been
written about in my earlier volumes on these subjects. These
autobiographical fragments are only part of the whole. But,
for me, the person and the place cannot be separated. Nor
can the time. It does not take many seconds of a present-day
summer's afternoon spent in a quiet garden, where the soft,
constant humming of insects is an acceptable accompaniment
to the stillness, to return in spirit to those long hot summers
of fifty years ago when, as a child, I stopped whatever I was
doing to listen to the pleasant drone of that year's insects. I
need only the fraction of a minute to be reminded of the
scents of flowers in gardens that have long since disappeared,
or to hear the distant ringing of bells to be back in a town
where bells were part of every day's pleasure. To see a boy
showing-off on his bicycle, or talking to himself as he
examines the latest addition to whatever it is he is collecting,
is a sufficient flame to the short fuse that detonates another
memory that has lain dormant for half a century.

Returning home across the fens a few weeks ago I stopped
the car and walked over to what is left of the little
railway-station, which is now no more than a halt for
two-car diesels or *Sprinter* trains on their way to Ely and
Cambridge. What platform there is cannot accommodate all
the ghosts who could gather there if I called to them. What
happened to the station clock, or the ticket office, or the row
of red fire-buckets that hung outside the gents? I stood and,
for a visionary moment, thought I saw a cocky boy in
open-neck shirt emerge from the mist and whack the
glistening air with his spade. I recognized the grin, recognized
too the blue-and-white beach-ball under his arm and his still
white plimsolls. He turned and appeared to speak to a
wraith-like porter who checked an invisible watch and, for an
immeasurable second, I thought I heard the sound of an
approaching train, a signal click, the song in the rails, the

flutter of excitement in my stomach at the prospect of another holiday. I wanted to speak but knew there was no point in getting any closer. As it was, a goods-train went noisily past and, when I looked again, there was no sign of anyone there, shadow or ghost. The smell of polish from the waiting-room had evaporated into the vacant air, the boy had gone on his way, back to the sea.

I returned to my car and made what I can only call a solemn procession past the recreation ground, the place where the blacksmith's was, the school playground and on to the market-place. I drove then down the street where I used to live and along the road where the old brickyards used to be.

It was like leaving home for the first – and indeed – the last time.